D0105318

To:

From:

Date:

365 Devotions to Embrace What Matters Most

By John W. Michalak

ZONDERVAN®

365 Devotions to Embrace What Matters Most

Copyright © 2015 by Zondervan

Requests for information should be addressed to:
Zondervan, Grand Rapids, Michigan 49530

ISBN 978-0-310-00358-8

Cover design: Kathy Mitchell
Interior design: Lori Lynch

Printed in China

15 16 17 18 19 20 TIMS 15 14 13 12 11 10 9 8 7 6 5 4 3 2

Introduction

Time can get away from us.

Sure, time can seem to muddle on forever—when we feel like a workday will never end or we're watching the clock in school, thinking the bell will never ring. But the older we get, the more we realize that minutes have become hours, days have become months, and years have become decades. Suddenly half of our lives has passed, and we wonder where the time went and, more important, how we actually spent that time.

Did we step out the door to see the world and discover its wonders? Or did we waste our time moving from one favorite television show to the next? Did we find out what we were called to do and push forward through obstacles such as tight finances, lack of education, or the desire to further refine our characters? Or did we allow fear or laziness to win the day, and spend our lives settling for jobs that left us less than inspired? Did we embrace the richness of close relationships and family? Or did we go from one superficial encounter to the next, running away when life got too messy? *Tick . . . tick . . . tick.*

If you're reading this, the clock hasn't stopped for you! As long as you're breathing in and breathing out, you still have time to make the rest of your life matter. And although the clock hasn't stopped, I would like *you* to stop. For a few moments each day, spend a little time meditating on the things that matter:

- who you are, why you're here, and what you should do about it.
- how you see the world.
- how to free yourself from the rat race.
- the importance of your relationships.
- what's wrong and how to make it right.
- how to become a better human being.

Think deeply about what really matters. Then take the necessary steps to begin embracing a life that matters.

PART 1:

WHO YOU ARE, WHY YOU'RE HERE, AND WHAT YOU SHOULD DO ABOUT IT!

YOU

Seven billion people live on this planet. Billions more have lived before us. But there has never been anyone exactly like you. You have a personality, a set of gifts, talents, and weaknesses all your own. You have a body size and shape, freckles, wrinkles, a nose, and eyes that set you apart from anyone who has ever lived.

You have a story that is unlike any other story. You've suffered; you have overcome. You've succeeded and you have failed. You've been hurt and you have hurt others. You are the hero of your story and sometimes the villain. No one has lived the life you've lived.

You are loved. You, personally. You, with all your habits and addictions, with all your judgments of others and of yourself. You. *You* are loved deeply and without reservation.

If you had never lived, the world would be the worse for it. You matter.

"I have loved you with an everlasting love; I have drawn you with unfailing kindness." —Jeremiah 31:3

Who You Are

What's your name? Though you can't answer me, it'd be wonderful to know. Specifically, your first name—your personal name.

Not your nickname. Nicknames, even if they describe something positive (and they rarely do), most often reveal only one part of us. They limit who we are to others and to ourselves.

Last names? At best, they describe only who our parents are, which could be good or bad. But they can also limit us in discovering our personal identities.

A first name is personal though. It is individual. It represents *you*.

Who you are matters, because how you identify yourself essentially determines the life you will live. It is the foundation for how you think, what you do, how you see the world, what kind of work you might pursue, or the kind of person you might marry.

So what *is* your name? It'd be wonderful to know.

They were going to name him after his father Zechariah, but his mother spoke up and said, "No! He is to be called John."
—*Luke 1:59–60*

Who You Are Becoming

Did you know that you are always changing?

Your body's molecules constantly renew themselves. The rate of change is much higher the younger you are and slows down as you grow older, but your body is always working on becoming something entirely different than it was before.

That adds a new layer to your identity. Not just to who you are, but to who you are *becoming*.

You are a character in a story that is still being written. Many people look at their lives and assume that who they were or who they are is all they will ever be. But the ultimate purpose of living is renewal. It is to gain *more* life.

Who you are becoming matters because you're meant for more.

What's your name again? And what do you think your new name might be? It'd be wonderful to know.

Jesus looked at him and said, "You are Simon son of John. You will be called Cephas" (which, when translated, is Peter). —John 1:42

Your Dreams

Most people forget their dreams.

Even the dreams you have just before waking—you might have a grasp of the details as you move from slumber to reality, but as you become more aware of the real world, the dream fades into the shadows of your subconscious.

Children are better than adults at playing with their dreams. "What do you want to be when you grow up?" "A pirate! A rich tycoon! An astronaut!" But then we grow up and stop pretending. We don't imagine or dream about what we could be.

We think that to make it in this world, we have to wake up and smell the coffee. And yes, by settling for the status quo, we'll make it from day to day. But will we truly live?

Close your eyes. Imagine the peace of slumber, letting go of the need to settle for what's expected.

Can you remember your dreams? They matter.

Now glory be to God, who by his mighty power at work within us is able to do far more than we would ever dare to ask or even dream of—infinitely beyond our highest prayers, desires, thoughts, or hopes. —Ephesians 3:20 TLB

Marching to Your Own Drummer

Y ou. Who you are. Who you are becoming. Your dreams. Don't let other people define you.

We want to belong, but we often allow this need for acceptance to shape us into something we're not. We jump off the Brooklyn Bridge because our friends did. We wear the clothes we wear because someone we've never met decided it's the latest fashion. To get ahead in life, we pine for attention from people who couldn't care less about us.

And we find that who we are has become defined by a follow-the-crowd mentality, a patchwork of people who've sold their souls for the meaningless illusion that they belong to something.

Remember, God loves you deeply and without reservation. So march to the beat of your own drummer.

It is for freedom that Christ has set us free. —Galatians 5:1

Who You Are to Those Who Matter

Have you ever seen a couple who have been married fifty years who almost look like brother and sister? How did *that* happen? You look at photos of their wedding and they didn't seem so similar back then. What changed?

Some fear losing their identities in marriage. But when you look at these long-married couples, they're still who they are, and yet they reflect the image of the person who has sat across the table from them all these years.

While who you are shouldn't depend on the whims of the majority or the tyrannies of fashion or fitting in, most people *are* meant to do life in community with others. And so while you're standing in your own shoes, your identity should also be defined by the relationships that matter:

Husband. Wife. Mother. Father. Son. Daughter. Friend. Created being. Reflecting the image of your Creator.

When God created mankind, he made them in the likeness of God.
—*Genesis 5:1*

Who You Are in Your Creator

Do you ever feel like you never quite measure up?
The little insecurities. The shame. The longing to know and be known. The striving after something . . . you don't know what. You feel unspoken expectations from family or teachers or bosses, wondering what more you can do to win their approval.

You face your days feeling adrift, separated from your roots. You find ways to avoid reality, running from who you are, because you feel so unworthy.

But you are not alone. You have been created, so you are connected to your Creator.

Who you are measures up because you came from the source of all that matters. You were created to matter.

Who are you? Perhaps what matters more is this question: Who are you *with*?

> But Moses said to God, "Who am I that I should go to Pharaoh and bring the Israelites out of Egypt?" And God said, "I will be with you." —Exodus 3:11–12

Why Are You Here?

Once there was a student sitting down to take his final exam in philosophy class. He expected a mountain of multiple choice and essay questions on the greatest thinkers and the most complicated theories he'd spent all semester studying.

He then opened his exam booklet and saw only three words:

"Why? Please explain."

After you consider your identity—*who* you are—the next question should be *why*?

Why are you here?

Why is the question that points to your purpose. Why were you born at this place and time? Why were you given certain talents, interests, desires? What are you meant to accomplish while here on planet Earth?

Why are you here? If you don't know, that's okay. But it's time to start studying because your final exam will arrive before you know it.

Why are you here? Please explain.

The purpose of life . . . is a life of purpose. —author unknown

Your Passions

Did you ever play the game where you must find a hidden object and another person gives you hints as to how close you are? They give clues: "Warm. Warmer. Colder. Warm. You're getting warmer . . ." And when you finally locate the object, you are burning up, absolutely on fire!

Your first step toward discovering why you are here is to follow your internal clues about the things that interest you (warmer) and the things that fill you with a sense of disinterest or dread (colder). Move toward the red-hot fires. These are your passions.

Your passions are desires, interests, or activities that are lit by an unquenchable flame. They burn deep. When you dwell on them, you feel an energy that drives and satisfies.

Your passions matter because they are your first and best clues to recognizing your life's purpose.

If your purpose is hidden, then seek out your passions. The closer you get, the more your life will begin to ignite.

When you set yourself on fire, people love to come and see you burn. —John Wesley

Your Talents

Elementary school productions are not to be missed. It's a celebration of organized chaos. Cute costumes, glassy-eyed looks of terror, some kids clearly bored, some experiencing perfectly timed meltdowns.

And the audience is chock-full of proud parents, video cameras in hand, zooming in on their child, documenting every detail like a reporter at the State of the Union Address.

Their kid may be flubbing every line, singing off-key, or not singing at all, but it doesn't matter. It's their kid, and she might as well be Meryl Streep or Pavarotti. No one on earth is like their kid, and that makes all the difference.

Your purpose shows up in your passions, and your passions surface in your talents. You may not be Streep or Pavarotti, but God is the parent zeroed in on your every move saying, "See there! That's my kid! What a talent!"

Your talents matter because no one else on earth has them. And the world needs what it does not have.

I praise you because I am fearfully and wonderfully made.
—Psalm 139:14

Your Architecture for Success

The Leaning Tower of Pisa is a remarkable structure. Its architecture is beautiful, and its storied lean is a gravity-defying flaw. Even with the efforts to stabilize its foundation, the fact that countless visitors have climbed its steps for hundreds of years without the tower crumbling to the ground is a mystery to the untrained observer.

As you build your life, perhaps your structure is also beautiful yet leaning, and some days you wonder how you don't just topple to the ground. Of course, your building is too genius to destroy, but your foundation may need some stabilization.

To succeed in living out your life's purpose, you need a blueprint from the Master Architect for what you were designed to be and do. Only He is best qualified to stabilize your foundation to ensure you remain standing.

Leaning perhaps, but tall and beautiful.

"For I know the plans I have for you," declares the LORD, "plans to prosper you and not to harm you, plans to give you hope and a future." —Jeremiah 29:11

Modeling Others

Have you ever played tennis and found yourself facing someone with a lightning-fast serve and a wicked volley? Most of us won't play someone much better than we are; it's no fun to have your pants beaten off every time you play.

If you're playing just for recreation and exercise, it's fine to only play others at or below your skill level. But if part of your goal is to become a better tennis player, matching your athletic wits against the local club pro is probably in your best interest.

Once you discover and start walking in your life's purpose, the next step is to place yourself under the tutelage of those who share a similar purpose, but are farther down the road in their journey.

You may get your pants beaten off, but you'll become a much better player.

As iron sharpens iron, so one person sharpens another.
—Proverbs 27:17

Trial and Error

The phrase *trial and error* can indicate possible failure, but may also signal a path to success.

We all love the comfort of the familiar, and stepping out to live your life's purpose is full of unknowns. It places you in the uncomfortable realm of trial and error.

But it's only in trying different ideas or pursuits—and risking that those ideas or pursuits could be mistakes—that you'll ever be able to flesh out and refine your purpose and discover where and how it should be applied.

You need to remain decisive and fully committed to this testing ground, no matter your fears. An untested purpose has no fortitude or integrity. Without trial and error, it will remain a straw man of good intentions.

We all make mistakes—try erring on the side of purpose.

The words of the LORD are flawless, like silver purified in a crucible, like gold refined seven times. —Psalm 12:6

Keeping Purpose Alive

Be on the lookout for purpose-killers.

They disguise themselves so they can ambush you. They may be obvious like laziness and procrastination. They could wear the masks of self-doubt and distraction.

If they're highly clever, they costume themselves in noble detours, such as the unending demands of work, family, church, and community obligations. These are areas of life that are good in and of themselves, but can drop you into a drain of excuses that keep you from living your life's purpose.

The things that really matter in this life are always a challenge to pursue and to maintain. That's why so many people—even while pursuing what is good—live lives without purpose. It's so much easier to stay on the simple path.

But once you discover and start living out your purpose, you must protect it from an untimely death at all costs.

All hard work brings a profit, but mere talk leads only to poverty.
—Proverbs 14:23

A Safe Place to Grow

Greenhouses are a safe haven for the growing plant. They're built to provide regulated temperatures, direct access to sunlight, ventilation, moisture—all the requirements needed for plants to transform from seed to bloom. As long as a plant is placed in the right environment and given the right stimuli and nutrients, growth is simply a matter of time.

As you pursue a life that matters, you need a safe place to grow. You need to avoid the elements that will stunt your growth, or worse, make your leaves wither and die. You need a place where it's safe to make mistakes and try again. To be who you are, good or bad. You need a place where your roots can find healthy soil and be fed, watered, and nurtured, a place where you'll have direct access to the light of life.

Once you've found this place, plant yourself there. Your growth is just a matter of time.

"Still other seed fell on good soil, where it produced a crop—a hundred, sixty or thirty times what was sown." —Matthew 13:8

The Seed

Living for what matters must start with a seed, an idea. It starts with understanding who you are and what your purpose is and knowing that you have some growing up to do.

In one sense, the seed is your vision for what lies ahead. Vision provides us with the needed courage and sense of direction to venture out into the unknown. Vision offers the promise that our growth will have a purpose, that it won't be wasted.

But as with any journey, where you start is not where you finish. The ideas you have about yourself and where you're going will most likely transform into something entirely different in the end.

The purpose of any seed is to die to itself, to grow up, and to bear life-giving fruit.

What you sow does not come to life unless it dies. When you sow, you do not plant the body that will be, but just a seed, perhaps of wheat or of something else. —1 Corinthians 15:36–37

Good Soil

Even the best vision for growth can be wasted when planted in the wrong soil.

If you plant yourself among those who don't understand or respect your desire to grow up into a life that matters, you may give up on growing.

If you're in an environment that's too superficial to have any roots in what matters, eventually you'll give up on growing.

If you plant yourself among those who pursue consumerism and meaningless pleasure, you'll stop growing and just give up.

Your seed must be planted in good soil, with those who are growing as well and are committed to your growth; a place where you can be rooted and grounded in love among those who are pursuing freedom away from the lures of superficial living.

Simply wanting to grow is not enough: good soil is everything.

"The seed on good soil stands for those with a noble and good heart, who hear the word, retain it, and by persevering produce a crop."
—Luke 8:15

Plant Food

I'll make a bet that you've never had to relearn that one plus one equals two.

You learned it in grade school and that was it. Check. You moved on to subtraction, multiplication, division, fractions, and perhaps into more advanced math such as algebra, geometry, and trigonometry.

While I'm sure you've learned many things, most of the time, you don't have to learn the same thing twice.

This isn't how you should approach your growth and maturity in what matters, however. Is knowledge and wisdom part of your growth? Of course. But the knowledge and wisdom you need is as much like good nutrition as it is sound instruction.

You might only need to learn something once, but if you eat only once, you'll die. You have to feed yourself regularly in order to grow strong.

"Man shall not live on bread alone, but on every word that comes from the mouth of God." —Matthew 4:4

Access to the Light

Sunlight is another form of food for plants. Perhaps you recall from science class that sunlight is converted by plants into chemical nutrients and helps the plant continue its growth. Plants don't need sunlight all the time, but a little is necessary for their growth and vitality.

People need sunlight too and suffer when they're deprived of it for long periods. You may be familiar with people living in places such as Alaska and Russia who suffer from what's called Seasonal Affective Disorder, a condition resulting from prolonged darkness. People with this disorder demonstrate such symptoms as deep depression, anger, and anxiety. Their systems essentially shut down and stop growing.

Light feeds us. It provides direction on an unknown path and prevents us from stumbling. It exposes what is harmful and unhealthy. It reveals the areas of life that matter.

If you want to grow, you need access to the light.

The people walking in darkness have seen a great light; on those living in the land of deep darkness a light has dawned. —Isaiah 9:2

You Need Love

Some babies are born prematurely and enter this world fighting for life.

About thirty years ago, doctors found a way to give such children a chance. They asked the mother to hold the preemie under her shirt for a prolonged period so the baby could have skin-to-skin contact.

The results were encouraging. The babies' heart rates and breathing stabilized, their weight increased, and they slept longer and cried less. And very often, mother and child could leave the hospital much earlier than cases without such intervention.

The rate and quality of your growth is dependent on love. You need to be nurtured and feel the warmth of other human beings who have a vested interest in your existence.

No matter how frail and helpless you may start out, there are those just waiting to love you back to life.

I pray that you, being rooted and established in love, may have power . . . to grasp how wide and long and high and deep is the love of Christ . . . that you may be filled to the measure of all the fullness of God. —Ephesians 3:17–19

Give It Time

W hen did you get so big?!"
These are the sometimes-annoying words we heard from aunts or grandmothers who came to visit from far away; people who hadn't seen us for some time and couldn't believe how much we'd grown.

One reason this was annoying was that, for us, the change was hardly noticeable. We didn't feel as if we grew! We were who we were.

In fact, the younger you are, the slower your growth seems to go. It feels like an eternity before you will ever be old enough to drive a car, get a job, travel the world.

Growth is a matter of time, and the watched pot never boils. When you choose to grow up and embrace a life that matters, it's important not to gauge your progress on just the good days or the bad days.

Give it time. Eventually, someone will show up to visit from far away and will gush over the difference.

Have patience with all things, but first of all with yourself.
—Saint Francis de Sales

Curiosity

What is out there? Is this all you are? What more do you have to learn?

Aren't you curious to know?

Learning should never stop for any of us, but too often it does. We spend our days as children bored to tears, loathing the thought of more homework, the next test, and dreading the idea of solving one more math problem.

Occasionally, we'll discover a subject that inspires us, and for some, this leads to college. But for many, learning tends to slow down when we reach adulthood. And with it ends any chance we might have to learn about what matters.

Identity. Purpose. Growth. Hopefully by now you've learned or rediscovered a few things that matter, and to do that you first needed to be curious.

Hopefully you're curious enough to discover what else you have to learn.

There's *always* more to learn.

Let the wise listen and add to their learning, and let the discerning get guidance. —Proverbs 1:5

Being Teachable

Often, in order to learn, you have to unlearn.

You live your life according to a certain set of assumptions, and if you come across a bit of wisdom that challenges those assumptions, your first instinct may be to resist the new information altogether.

Of course, not every new piece of knowledge will be true, healthy, or worth following. But if you adopt the assumption that there is more for you to learn, a follow-up to that is admitting that some of what you now know could be wrong, or at the very least, could stand to be tweaked.

Here's something I bet you do know: not everything in your life is working. And when you know something's wrong and are not sure how to make it right, you need to be open to new solutions, new ideas that may challenge your thinking—and perhaps your behavior.

You need to be teachable.

Blessed are those who find wisdom, those who gain understanding.
—Proverbs 3:13

Understanding

Have you ever listened to someone mentioning people or facts you don't recognize, but you still nod your head as if you know what they're saying? You pray that they'll soon move on to another topic before they ask what you think and expect an intelligent answer.

In most cases like this, it's not terribly important to understand. But if you're lost in a strange city without your GPS and need to ask for directions, understanding exactly how many blocks there are before turning right on Elm becomes more vital to fully grasp. In this case, you are more motivated to pay close attention and write it all down.

Perhaps it goes without saying, but learning about what matters requires a devotion to paying close attention, to understanding what you hear.

Especially if you find yourself in need of good direction.

Then Philip . . . heard the man reading Isaiah the prophet. "Do you understand what you are reading?" Philip asked. "How can I," he said, "unless someone explains it to me?" So he invited Philip to come up and sit with him. —Acts 8:30—31

Going Deep

It's a lot easier to live life on the surface.

You can float around and allow the current to take you where it will. To dive underneath the water takes some gumption. You have to hold your breath and adjust your vision. And the deeper you dive, the more pressure you feel. Even at the bottom of a ten-foot pool, the pressure feels immense, forcing most people back to the surface.

But learning about a life that matters is like diving for treasure that rests on the ocean floor. You have to leave the comforts of surface living and endure the pressure of the deep in order to reap the rewards of something valuable.

For surface-dwellers, a life that matters is too deep and too difficult to pursue.

But now that you know the treasure's down there, you'd be crazy not to start learning how to dive.

If you . . . search for [understanding] as for hidden treasure, then you will understand the fear of the LORD and find the knowledge of God. —Proverbs 2:4—5

Aha Moments

Have you ever watched the show *Are You Smarter Than a 5th Grader?* There is something entertaining about watching these adults, many of whom are educated professionals, who can't remember the basic facts of fourth-grade history or fifth-grade biology.

The amount you've learned and forgotten could probably fill a library. But for every fact you've forgotten, it's likely you can still recall the lessons that matter most. These could be called the *aha moments*, where something your heard or experienced pierced your heart and you felt enlightened.

Maybe a teacher once pulled you aside and taught you a life lesson you've never forgotten. Maybe you sat with a friend over coffee and something they said struck you like a lightning bolt. Maybe God spoke to you in the deep hours of the night and you were never the same. Perhaps you'll encounter a few reading this book.

Be ready for the *aha* moments. They matter.

I pray that the eyes of your heart may be enlightened.
—*Ephesians 1:18*

Application

Why *should* you learn anything else?

Just because there's more to learn? Some would say yes. But then you'll be really smart with nothing to show for it. Gaining knowledge just for the sake of knowing more is an exercise in vanity. Learning about what matters must lead somewhere.

But it's a good guess that this isn't the first book you've ever read about something that matters. Did you live it out? Did you apply what you learned from the other books?

The reason these questions are important is because many of us live our lives intoxicated by our good intentions. We read book after book about things that matter and never actually do anything.

Experience will be your best teacher. If you really want to learn about what matters, be prepared to *do* what matters.

But whoever looks intently into the perfect law that gives freedom, and continues in it—not forgetting what they have heard, but doing it—they will be blessed in what they do. —James 1:25

Receiving Correction

Road signs are usually helpful. They give you direction, they tell you the speed limit, and they alert you to areas of caution ahead.

The sign you probably least want to see says, Do Not Enter: Wrong Way. If you see such a sign, chances are you're traveling in the wrong direction and need to take quick action to avoid being mowed down by oncoming traffic.

Nobody likes to receive correction. It's embarrassing. Most often, we simply don't want to believe we need correcting. We get defensive. We blame others. We accuse the person addressing our error.

Remember: learning is also about unlearning, and it's unlikely that our journey to what matters won't include a few potholes and errant turns onto one-way streets.

So take a deep breath. Understand you're human. And simply turn around and head in the right direction.

Those who disregard discipline despise themselves, but the one who heeds correction gains understanding. Wisdom's instruction is to fear the LORD, and humility comes before honor.
—Proverbs 15:32—33

What Is Wisdom?

Wisdom is your future self coming to visit you in a time machine.

If you could travel back in time, what would you tell yourself? You'd probably have a list of lessons you had to learn the hard way. You'd have cautionary tales about how to avoid future pitfalls and silly mistakes.

Wisdom is just that: bits of knowledge that will help to keep you from living foolishly.

Some mistakes we make in life are because we just don't know any better. Sometimes we know what to do, but walk down the wrong path over and over, and never learn our lesson. Sometimes, we're so full of pride that no one can tell us anything.

Wisdom looks into your future to tell you where your actions will lead.

Wisdom can save you from an unfulfilled life.

Out in the open wisdom calls aloud. . . . "How long will mockers delight in mockery and fools hate knowledge? Repent at my rebuke! Then I will pour out my thoughts to you, I will make known to you my teachings." —Proverbs 1:20, 22–23

Guidance

The time machine hasn't been invented yet, but there's still probably someone who *can* visit you from the future to help you pursue a life that matters.

Anyone who has been down the road you're traveling can help you avoid its pitfalls.

A lot of people have advice, but you need people with a track record for wise thinking and, more importantly, wise behavior. Grandparents. Teachers. Pastors. Counselors. Mentors. Seek out a friend who has at least twenty years on you and pursue them until they tell you all their secrets for living well.

A lot of wise people have written books. Use them as guides. God is pretty wise and He wrote a book.

The whole point is for these principles to make your life better. The best proof will be found in people who've lived them out and are better for it.

Do you want to be wise? Spend time with people who have lived a life that matters.

Follow my example, as I follow the example of Christ.
—*1 Corinthians 11:1*

What Is Right

We live in a world where it's not polite to be right. If you are right, then somebody else is wrong, and that's just bad manners.

And although we should walk in humility and respect for others when we disagree, that doesn't mean there is no right and wrong.

Most people agree that murder is wrong. Most frown on adultery. The abuse of children? That's not right. Injustices occur every day, and these need to be righted.

But what about the less dramatic areas? Is it wrong to fudge a bit on your taxes? How about talking behind your friend's back? Is it right to max out your credit card on stuff you don't need?

Sometimes when we are reluctant to hold others to standards of right and wrong, we also let ourselves off the hook.

Without wisdom, you'll stray from a life that matters. And wisdom requires the pursuit of what is right.

If you accept my words . . . turning your ear to wisdom . . . then you will understand what is right and just and fair—every good path. —Proverbs 2:1–2, 9

Discernment

Is there right and wrong? That's one question. What is right and what is wrong? That's another. Answering these questions requires discernment.

Again, for most people, the big-ticket issues like murder and abuse are easy to decide upon. But you won't typically encounter these issues in your daily life. You will encounter smaller challenges, like cheating on your diet or gossip. Why are the smaller areas important? Because small compromises can collect like coins in a jar, adding up over time.

Hopefully you're starting to get a sense of who you are, why you're here, and that you need to grow up again and learn new solutions to what's not working. Wisdom will be your safeguard to pursuing such a life, but it will require recognizing that some of the areas we call *gray* are very often black and white to those with better glasses.

Seek guidance. Commit to pursuing what is right. And improve your vision to discern what it is.

Solid food is for the mature, who by constant use have trained themselves to distinguish good from evil. —Hebrews 5:14

Caution

You can only run a stop sign so many times.

Perhaps you feel familiar with the intersection. It's quiet and there's rarely any cross traffic.

You do come to a full stop at first. But on your next trip you don't quite stop; you move slowly into the intersection, looking both ways. On future trips, you relax even more until eventually, you enter the intersection looking straight ahead and barely slow down at all.

Smack! What just happened? Did you have an accident? *To be honest, officer, I never saw it coming.*

Wisdom looks ahead to the end of your actions. It improves your focus to discern between right and wrong, between good choices and bad.

In this spirit, wisdom advises you to be cautious. To be on the lookout for unseen dangers.

Wisdom is smarter than all of us. And when wisdom says *stop before moving forward*, you should listen.

For wisdom will enter your heart, and knowledge will be pleasant to your soul. —Proverbs 2:10

Experience Necessary

One benefit of pursuing wisdom is that you don't always have to learn from experience. You can save time by avoiding poor choices when you follow its sage advice.

However, experience is still a great teacher.

Experiencing mistakes can be a strong motivator to turn toward wise living. The sting and consequences of past mistakes can be the foundation you always needed to fully commit to a life that matters.

Gaining wisdom, like learning, isn't just about scratching your chin and mulling over cryptic philosophies. It's about living. And you have to step out and *live* wisdom, placing yourself in the trenches of hard choices between right and wrong, to truly become wiser.

What you learn from wisdom might help you to avoid suffering the consequences of foolish living. But as long as you recognize the opportunity to learn from experience, wisdom will win either way.

If you are wise, your wisdom will reward you. —Proverbs 9:12

Counselors

The President of the United States doesn't know everything. He has years of experience in governing, but he doesn't have the wisdom to understand every issue the nation is facing or to discern what is right and wrong in every hard choice coming across his desk.

So a wise president surrounds himself with wise counselors. He'll consult experts in foreign policy, the military, economics, politics, and communication. He'll make the final decisions, but he will ensure that those decisions are informed by multiple advisory boards.

In the same way that you need guidance from one wise friend or mentor, you'll also want to surround yourself with experts in the things that matter. Some will be wise in love. Some in choosing a career. Some will offer wisdom in how to heal or how to let go.

Ultimately, you'll make the final decisions, but be humble enough to shape those decisions through the wisdom that surrounds you.

Without counsel, plans go awry, but in the multitude of counselors they are established. —Proverbs 15:22 NKJV

Productivity

Retirement is for suckers.

Did you know that even with advancements in medicine, the average person in the United States lives only about twelve years after they retire? True, the retirement age often coincides with the frailty of years, but that seems like too short a time to live beyond working for a living. Why is this?

When some retire, they don't just stop working, they stop producing. Remember that you were created for a purpose, and that purpose is most often carried out through what you produce. People who no longer produce lose their purpose, and people without a purpose aren't truly alive. And eventually your physical body catches up with that reality.

But the word is *produce*, not work. Productivity is more than just your job or career. You want to produce a life and a legacy that matters. And you can do that long after your first Social Security check arrives.

> *Preparation for old age should begin not later than one's teens. A life which is empty of purpose until 65 will not suddenly become filled on retirement.* —Dwight L. Moody

Working for What Matters

Have you spent years working at a factory or behind a desk and wondered what you were achieving? Many will settle for an occupation that does little to inspire them. If that's you, perhaps you should take a look at who you are and what your purpose is and follow your dreams to work for what matters.

However, if working at a factory or behind a desk has provided a roof over your head for you and your family, allowed you to put your kids through school, and enabled you to volunteer at church or in your community, then what you do for a living matters.

If you're a mom who spends most of your time at home raising your children and managing the household, you are also working for what matters.

But no matter what you do day to day, don't just work to make a living. Work to produce a life. A life that both supports and is built upon what matters.

Rise up; this matter is in your hands. We will support you, so take courage and do it. —Ezra 10:4

Hard Work

Despite what you've seen on TV, life has no easy button. Too many people have been lulled into the slumber of instant gratification. We've forgotten the basic rule handed down from our elders: what matters in life requires work—and usually hard work.

It is work to exercise, to eat right, and to keep yourself fit. It is hard work to keep a house clean, to care for infants and teenagers, to be a good spouse. It is work to come up with fresh ideas, to be diligent with your studies, to go to church, to pray, to volunteer in your community.

Hard work matters because there needs to be a correlation between what you have and how much work was done to produce it. Otherwise, you'll disintegrate into selfishness, and what you have won't matter. You'll incessantly crave more and will be left with nothing.

The TV is lying to you: life is often difficult. Be willing to work hard for the life that matters.

The soul of the sluggard craves and gets nothing, while the soul of the diligent is richly supplied. —Proverbs 13:4 ESV

Quality

Have you ever seen the intricate and gorgeous detail in Shaker-made furniture?

Most active during the nineteenth century, the Shakers were a community known not just for quality furniture, but also for ingenious inventions such as the circular saw and the washing machine. They are also known for eye-popping architecture, glorious music and literature, rich agriculture, and a joyful communal life.

The Shakers were connected to the quality of God's work in creation. So the focus of their work and life was to reflect a similar level of quality and excellence in whatever they put their hands to.

As you discover your identity, your purpose, and how the life that matters calls you to grow, learn, and become wiser, you'll realize that all is a reflection of the quality work of your Creator—and that what you do in life can no longer be about settling for *good enough*.

You yourself are an intricate, gorgeous work of art. Raise the bar on what you do to reflect who you are.

Whatever your hand finds to do, do it with all your might.
—*Ecclesiastes 9:10*

Teamwork

The elements of nature work well together. Ants and bees are famous for their coordinated efforts. Birds fly faster in formation. Wolves hunt best in packs. The wind helps pollinate plants and flowers.

Really, most things that matter are the product of multiple parts working together to produce a unified whole—from the working parts in any machine to the miraculous factory called the human body.

Sometimes the best way to get the job done is to work alone. But if that's the only way you work, your productivity will be limited. Depend on the support and cooperation of others, especially those with skills you don't have. Others with perspectives and ideas with which you may not always agree.

You too are a creation of the natural order. Consider what could be produced if you functioned as a part and not the whole.

Two are better than one, because they have a good return for their labor: If either of them falls down, one can help the other up. But pity anyone who falls and has no one to help them up.
—Ecclesiastes 4:9–10

Be Contagious

In working for what matters, the ultimate end of your productivity should be *REproductivity*.

Raise children who will follow in your footsteps and grow up to pursue what matters themselves. Raise them to become parents who'll want do the same for their children.

Don't just work on your marriage: love well, forgive, stick it out because you know your marriage isn't just about you. You can set an example so others will want a marriage that matters.

If you have a job, show up on time, apply yourself, be flexible, be kind to others. Encourage those around you to take pride in their work and to walk in integrity. Encourage them to train others to do likewise.

It's hard work to live as an example. But to work for what matters means your life should matter to those around you. Produce a life that is contagious to others.

Be fruitful . . . multiply on the earth and increase upon it.
—Genesis 9:7

What Is Finished

You should never retire from or give up on producing a life that matters. In that sense, your job will never be finished. But that doesn't mean your journey will have no benchmarks, no victories, no sense of accomplishment along the way.

Your child comes home with an A on the homework that you worked on together. The friend you've been spending hours on the phone counseling calls back to say that she is going to try to work things out with her spouse. Your kid graduates college. You finally pay off the mortgage. You renew your wedding vows after forty years of marriage.

What you produce *will* have results. You *will* bear fruit. But after one task is finished, another will begin. Until your last breath, until you are truly finished with this life, more will always await you.

Your journey never ends. Life has a way of changing things in incredible ways. —author unknown

More

More matters.

Who you are, why you're here, and what you should do about it must always be driven by the truth that there is so much more to life than you ever imagined.

You're not unlike the unsuspecting hero being asked to step out on an adventure. There you were, quietly living your life, when suddenly you were called to go on a quest. There's too much at stake! Something needs to be done, and you must come along and play your part.

The life that matters requires that you step out beyond what's familiar into the unknown, perilous, exhilarating land of More.

Should you go back to school and get that degree? The downtown homeless shelter looks scary. Should you stop by and volunteer? You're tired of not having friends. Maybe you should accept that invitation to your coworker's church picnic. Maybe you could talk to someone about getting free from your addiction.

And there's more. There's so much more . . .

"I have come that they may have life, and that they may have it more abundantly." —*John 10:10 NKJV*

What You Fear

Fear can be a healthy emotion. You should fear crossing the street without looking both ways. You should fear loose mountain lions, tornado warnings, and smoking five packs of cigarettes a day.

But fear can also keep you from leaving what's familiar to experience this life of adventure. When you ignore *these* kinds of fears, you'll find yourself only dreaming of adventure and never actually living it.

Am I good enough? Can I do it? What will it be like? What if I fail? What if I get hurt again?

Naming your fears can make them feel a little less threatening. But once they're named, they must be banished, or at least muted. The adventures you've been called to experience are more significant than your fears.

And more importantly, the One who calls you to step out the door believes you can do it, and He will guide you and protect you.

> *The word of the LORD came to Abram in a vision: "Do not be afraid, Abram. I am your shield, your very great reward."*
> *—Genesis 15:1*

Stepping Out the Door

You'll never know unless you do it.

In front of you stands the door between the life you know and some unknown change or adventure. You've prepared for the journey. Perhaps you've studied what the new opportunity will be like. Maybe you've asked others who have stepped out on a similar adventure before.

But now, maybe you're just stalling . . .

Of all the challenges a new pursuit or experience will present to you, few will be more menacing than the resistance taking place right between your ears. Everything within you will try to entice you to turn around, slip back into the recliner, and return to business as usual.

But you've been called by a new name. You've felt the fire of your life's purpose. You know that there's more for you to discover, to experience, to create.

Do it. Step forward. More is out there. Unless you go . . .

. . . you'll never know.

The Lord had said to Abram, "Go from your country, your people and your father's household to the land I will show you."
—*Genesis 12:1*

Traveling Companions

Once you step out on the road, people will likely join you on your adventure.

They've been called out themselves. They had to overcome their fears and step out their own doors. Some people you meet may not be heading in the same direction. But you should welcome the company of the ones who are.

Maybe you meet someone at your first college class and she becomes your study partner. You tell a friend about your visit to the homeless shelter and he asks if he can go with you next time. You meet a couple at the church picnic who invite you to their house for dinner. Someone at your recovery meeting looks at you with understanding eyes, offers you a cup of coffee, and sits down with you to listen.

The unknowns are still the unknowns. But the journey feels safer and more doable when someone starts walking with you.

They help each other and say to their companions, "Be strong!"
—Isaiah 41:6

Navigating Obstacles

No adventure story is without obstacles.

You will encounter dangers, distractions, and delays—things that will hinder you from reaching your goal.

You've done well in school, but then you start a new class and it's all you can do to make a passing grade. One of the homeless men you've made progress with disappears and doesn't show up for that job interview you arranged. You had several outings with that new couple, but now you wonder if you're just a third wheel. You stop answering when your sponsor calls and have a moment of relapse.

Forces in this world, and some within you, don't want you to succeed. They will block you, make you stumble, and try to break your determination to keep moving forward.

But ask yourself: How badly do you want to reach your goal? And what are you willing to do to get it?

No one can make you quit the adventure but you.

If you can find a path with no obstacles, it probably doesn't lead anywhere. —author unknown

All Is Lost

You failed that class. How will you graduate? The homeless man is now in jail and doesn't know when he'll get out. You cherish your friendship with that couple, but you just heard they're getting a divorce. You've had stretches of victory over your addiction, but just can't seem to break free.

Every adventure has an *all is lost* moment when the bottom drops out and it seems there is nowhere to turn.

The right thing to do may depend on your circumstances. Reach out to your traveling companions for support. Because they're on a similar adventure, few will encourage you like they can.

Always pray.

And know this: there is a great deal of freedom in helplessness. When you've run out of options, you're finally free, with a whole heart, to reach out for the One who can rescue you when no one else can.

"In my distress I called to the LORD, and he answered me. From deep in the realm of the dead I called for help, and you listened to my cry." —Jonah 2:2

Resolution

After *all is lost*, there is often *new hope*. Some discovery provides new energy to complete the journey. Then the package is wrapped up with a tidy bow—evil is vanquished and final victory is achieved. We have resolution.

Of course, your adventures probably won't end so neatly.

You'll still graduate, but you have to get a tutor and repeat the class first. You've had some good visits with the man in jail, and you meet another homeless woman who is interested in finding work. Your friends divorce, but you're a listening ear to both in their suffering. You finally agree to meet your sponsor for coffee.

There will someday be a final victory and resolution to our adventures. But for now, it's enough that we step out the door to join others on the road, refuse to give up, and press forward on to the next adventure.

Press on toward more.

But one thing I do: Forgetting what is behind and straining toward what is ahead, I press on toward the goal to win the prize for which God has called me heavenward in Christ Jesus.
—Philippians 3:13–14

PART 2:

HOW YOU SEE THE WORLD

Seeing What Matters

Viktor Frankl was a Jewish psychiatrist held captive in the Nazi concentration camps during World War II. In his book, *Man's Search for Meaning*, he describes how the Nazis stripped each person of their humanity—horrible living conditions, little food, unbearable labor, physical abuse, and the constant threat of death.

How he stayed alive when others died may seem miraculous. His circumstances were about the worst they could be. He had no control over his life. But he did have control over one thing.

His perspective.

No one could take from him the freedom to choose his attitude, or how he chose to see the world. When he had nothing else left, what mattered was his freedom to choose his perspective. And that gave him a reason to live.

What do you see when you look at your world? You can choose to see what matters.

"Blessed are your eyes because they see, and your ears because they hear." —Matthew 13:16

Climbing the Skyscraper

Imagine you're on a street corner in a large city. Cars zoom by. People are rushing. Concrete buildings loom above.

Now imagine you ride an elevator to the top of a skyscraper and look out over the roof. The world's much bigger. You can see beyond the city. Forests. Mountains. And the sun shining on everything.

Too often, we see things only from the street level. The baby won't stop crying. You're down with another flu bug. You're overdrawn at the bank. These aren't problems that should be ignored, but you can choose how you see them.

From atop of the skyscraper, how big are those problems? They're just a small part of the larger landscape that reaches to your life's horizon.

Sometimes you'll need help raising your perspective to enjoy such a view. But it's your choice to leave the street corner and step into the elevator.

I lift up my eyes to the mountains—where does my help come from?
—Psalm 121:1

A Nice Pair of Bifocals

A racecar driver was once asked how he avoided wrecks. He said that if you're looking down to the next turn as much as you're looking at what's right in front of you, you'll be able to both get ahead of other cars and also spot trouble before it arrives on your bumper.

You're not guaranteed your next breath. You could meet your maker in the next minute or in fifty years. So pay attention to what's right in front of you. See life as if you had little time to make the most of it, but also look ahead and plan your life as if you have decades more to reach for what matters.

Looking near and far at the same time may seem tough at first, but you can do it.

Buy a nice pair of bifocals.

These people were still living by faith when they died. They did not receive the things promised; they only saw them and welcomed them from a distance. —Hebrews 11:13

Objects Are Closer Than They Appear

Here's another visual balancing act to consider. When you're driving, you don't just look forward. You also look back. You lift your head to look into the rearview mirror. You shift your eyes back and forth to the side mirrors. You twist your head to look for blind spots. This helps you when changing lanes, and it helps you in adjusting your speed to remain at a safe distance from other cars.

But what would happen if you spent more time looking backward than forward? You might, by some chance, make it a little way. But pretty quickly, you'd crash.

Too often, our attention is stuck on the rearview mirror. The objects from our past, while they appear to be years behind, have a much closer hold on our hearts and minds than we realize.

Looking back *is* necessary for moving forward. Just remember to spend far more time looking in the direction you're heading.

But my eyes are fixed on you, Sovereign Lord. —Psalm 141:8

Seeing What Is Temporary

It's important not to make an eternity out of a temporary feeling.

You know the days. It's all you can do to get out of bed. You are so depressed, so hopeless about the world, that absolutely nothing matters.

We all go there sometimes. For some, it's physical and requires medication. Others feel like they were hit with a big rig, and nobody should blame them for feeling paralyzed by its blows. In that light, resist anyone who lobs clichés such as, "Turn that frown upside down!" or "Suck it up and get back in the game!"

But just like seeing your problems from a higher perspective makes them seem smaller, so it is that, although everything in you says that this feeling will never end, you can discipline your mind to hold on to the truth that it is only temporary.

Your job is simply to hold on. Morning is coming.

[The LORD's] compassions never fail. They are new every morning; great is your faithfulness. I say to myself, "The LORD is my portion; therefore I will wait for him."
—Lamentations 3:22–24

Seeing What Is Permanent

It is nice to know that some things never change.

Old men still wear their pants too high. Grandmothers still hug kids tightly. Small towns will always seem quaint. They'll always sell Peeps at Easter.

When you're overwhelmed by the whirlwind of work deadlines, soccer carpools, and endless laundry, it's nice to remember that there is a permanence to life, a foundation to hold on to when life's slipping from your grasp.

But here's the thing: grandmas, kids, and candy only go so far, and you'll still be left hungering for more. If this life is permanent—if this is all there is—then eventually the chaos around us will win.

If you're willing to see with different eyes, to see a permanence beyond what is seen, you'll discover a foundation for life that matters.

Our light and momentary troubles are achieving for us an eternal glory that far outweighs them all. So we fix our eyes not on what is seen, but on what is unseen, since what is seen is temporary, but what is unseen is eternal. —2 Corinthians 4:17–18

What Does Not Disappoint

So what was the perspective Viktor Frankl chose that helped him endure? What did he choose to focus on?

Hope.

Frankl entered the camps with his beloved wife, but they were separated. And he could never be sure what happened to her. So if there was someone out there who loved him and whom he loved in return, he had a reason to live. His faith in this little uncertainty gave him hope.

You too can cling to this little uncertainty.

If there is even the smallest possibility that there is a God out there who deeply loves every stitch of your existence, then you can have a hope that will never disappoint.

Like Frankl, you have the freedom to choose your perspective. No matter how trapped you are in your circumstances, you have the freedom to hope.

We . . . glory in our sufferings, because . . . suffering produces perseverance; perseverance, character; and character, hope. And hope does not put us to shame, because God's love has been poured out into our hearts through the Holy Spirit. —Romans 5:3—5

Zeroing In

When using a camera, you need to consider your focus if you want a good, clear photo.

First you need to decide the frame of your shot, what will be included in the picture and what will be left out. Then you must use your zoom, pinpoint in your view-finder what will be the center of the image, and adjust the focus so the most important part of what you're viewing becomes clear.

While it is related to perspective, or how you see the world, focus is more about *what* you choose to see and how clearly you see it. In other words, the ideas, people, or circumstances you choose to zero in on.

The problem isn't learning how to focus, exactly. I guarantee that you spend your days focusing on some-thing, likely many things. The trick is to learn how to focus on what matters and also to train your focus so you're better prepared to live the life that matters.

Set your minds on things above, not on earthly things.
—*Colossians 3:2*

Eye Candy

At the county fair, your eyes zoom in on the sign: Cotton Candy. This billowy confection forms around a cardboard cone. You pull off the first bite like you're plucking fruit off the finest tree. A rush of pleasure bursts on your taste buds before melting into nothing.

And nothing it is. While it appears to have size and substance, promising a world of delight, it's mostly air and a few grains of sugar.

As an occasional indulgence, such eye candy is fine. But for many of us, it's more than just occasional.

Your eyes are always drawn to who's divorcing whom on the magazine rack. You're obsessed with how your favorite team is doing. You can't wait to see which reality-show housewife goes off the rails next.

You are what you eat. Likewise, you tend to resemble what you most look upon. Resolve in your mind that you'll spend more of your time focusing on what matters.

Beware lest you lose the substance by grasping at the shadow.
—Aesop

Zoom Out

Imagine you're in a slow-moving car on safari in the Serengeti of Africa. Everywhere you look, there is wildlife—lions, elephants, zebras, giraffes, antelopes . . . you name it.

From a safe distance, you zoom in on a pride of lions with your camera and take several shots. But the lions, not surprisingly, are probably a fair distance away from many of the other animals. While your focus is in this tight, panning your viewfinder to the left or right won't help you find them. To zoom in on the giraffes or elephants, you'll first need to zoom out.

The focus of your heart and mind works in much the same way. Perhaps you've said that you'd like to start focusing on the things that matter. But the problem is, you're already focused on the things that don't.

So before you can zero in on what matters, you first need to zoom out, take in the larger landscape, and go in search of new animals.

Finally, brothers and sisters, whatever is true, whatever is noble, whatever is right, whatever is pure, whatever is lovely, whatever is admirable—if anything is excellent or praiseworthy—think about such things. —Philippians 4:8

The Still Shot

There is nothing like capturing a moment in time.

Many prefer the visual medium of movies, television, or home video. There's action, movement; a story is often told from beginning to end.

But a still shot? There's a story there too. You just have to pause to appreciate it.

The frozen moment of pure joy on your child's face as she soars on a swing . . . The tender look of intimacy as a couple steals a glance at their daughter's wedding reception . . . The eternal look of pride in a father's eyes as he poses with his son after his first football game . . .

Too often, our lives are a blur because we try to place our focus on far too many things at once when our camera is meant to focus on only one object at a time. Even when we're trying to focus on what matters, life might not have total clarity.

Appreciate the beauty of a moment in time. Then you can move on to the next.

Let your eyes look straight ahead; fix your gaze directly before you.
—Proverbs 4:25

How to Climb a Mountain

Hiking in the mountains is no easy task, even for the young. In fact, more than one young person has found him- or herself going up at a quick pace, only to fall out while the slower hikers pass by.

And that's the key: slow and steady wins the race. The trained hiker will often move at a snail's pace, eyes down, focused on the ground, moving one step at a time. That's how you climb a mountain.

What are your mountains? Losing weight? Training for a new career? Bringing healing to a broken relationship? The mountain feels so high that you almost want to quit before you even start.

You'll make it, but your focus must be on the step right in front of you. That's what you need to worry about—and nothing else. After that step, a new step will follow. Slow and steady. One step at a time.

That's how you climb a mountain.

"Therefore do not worry about tomorrow, for tomorrow will worry about itself. Each day has enough trouble of its own."
—Matthew 6:34

Take Off the Lens Cap

This may have happened to you at one time or another . . .
You're using your favorite camera, happily looking
through the viewfinder to take a photo, and then you hear
someone shout, "Take off the lens cap!" You assumed you
were focusing in on the subject, but something was block-
ing the camera's true eye all along.

Sometimes we can assume we're focusing on what
matters, but we are really taking pictures with the lens
cap on. How? By focusing too much on the behavior and
opinions of others while ignoring a significant blind
spot, or lens cap—the ownership we should take for our
own behavior.

We impose unnecessary judgments on others. We
blame everyone else for our problems. We don't see the
log in our own eye. Sometimes we first need to focus on
what we're blind to before we can focus on what matters.

*"You hypocrite, first take the plank out of your own eye, and then
you will see clearly to remove the speck from your brother's eye."*
—Matthew 7:5

Preventive Maintenance

The car is always in the shop. You can't see your desk through the mountain of paperwork. You seem to be buying more and more with the credit card. You're always arguing with your loved one about one issue or another.

You're living in crisis management. Your focus is always drawn to putting out little fires. Focusing on what matters is the last thing you could imagine doing.

But consider that your car wouldn't break down as much if you regularly changed the oil. Perhaps a few late nights are needed to sort through all that paperwork. Maybe it's time to sit down and write out a budget. Maybe it's time for a weekly date night and a few weekend getaways.

Although it may require a shift in behavior and some sacrifice, focusing on preventive maintenance will free you to focus more on the life the matters.

The plans of the diligent lead to profit as surely as haste leads to poverty. —Proverbs 21:5

Embracing Reality

The Greek philosopher Plato tells a story of people held prisoner in a cave from birth. They're bound head to toe so that all they can see is a wall. Behind them is a fire. Behind the fire, the cave entrance. Beyond the cave, the sun.

Outside the cave, people walk by. Those outside and the prisoners themselves cast shadows on the wall. So for those held prisoner inside the cave, people or anything related to reality are merely shadows of reality.

At first when they are freed from their bonds, they have a hard time believing it. They walk outside and see what is real, assuming that this vision must be illusion, that surely the shadows are what is true. But the shadows are, at best, once removed from reality.

Pursuing a life that matters means being freed from the cave and the shadows we've accepted as real, to see the world as it was meant to be seen.

To live life as it was meant to be lived.

Open my eyes that I may see. —Psalm 119:18

Shadows of the Real

Have you ever seen a counterfeit fifty-dollar bill? You probably have and never knew it.

To the untrained eye, a counterfeit bill looks exactly like the genuine article. You have to know what to look for to spot the difference.

Lust is mistaken for love. Vanity is mistaken for self-confidence. Materialism for security. Substance abuse for pleasure. Career for purpose. Overeating for nourishment. Entertainment for joy.

But hear some good news: if you've found yourself obsessed with any of these counterfeits or shadows, realize that 1) you're not alone, and 2) the basic need you're seeking to fill is a need that comes from the very heart of God.

God wants you to have things such as love, self-confidence, security, pleasure, purpose, nourishment, and joy, but they are waiting for you outside the cave.

Why not turn around and see?

"Why spend money on what is not bread, and your labor on what does not satisfy? Listen, listen to me, and eat what is good, and you will delight in the richest of fare." —Isaiah 55:2

Adjusting to the Light

Imagine you are one of those released from a life of seeing only shadows and are able turn and face reality. At first, you turn to face the fire and the sun, and you're barely able to see for the pain of the light. Your eyes are only used to the shadows, and the light is difficult to adjust to.

As you move from shadows to reality, you may initially feel a sense of insecurity and even blindness. For a time, you'll feel that you are worse off than you were before, that you can't function, certainly that you can't make sense of what's around you.

But what's real won't matter if you can't see it for what it is. You need the light both to reveal what is truly real and to dispel the shadows you've mistaken for reality. Be prepared for a time of transition when you may experience some pain and confusion.

Eventually, your eyes will adjust and you'll see everything you need to see.

"I was blind but now I see!" —John 9:25

Recognizing What Is Real

An energy drink will give you a surge of alertness and drive to conquer the world. That may last a few hours. After that, your body is back to its tired, passive state. If you need to be up again, you'll need another dose.

Water isn't as exciting. It's tasteless, and although you may feel better after a glass, it doesn't provide the same effect as the energy drink.

But water is real. It comes from God's creation and isn't the product of man's meddling. That's what your body really needs. Drinking water each day will give you energy and balance that can last years, not just a few fleeting hours.

How do you spot what's real? It's usually sourced in creation and made by our Creator. It isn't as attractive or quick-acting as its counterfeit. But by moving nearer to the source, you'll more readily recognize what really matters.

Who is wise? Let them realize these things. Who is discerning? Let them understand. —Hosea 14:9

What Is Truth?

Reality is probably a better word for truth.

When testimony in a court of law is called *truthful*, we say that it is an accurate testimony, a trustworthy account. And yes, that's true. But what we're really saying is that the words of the witness reflect *reality*, or what can be confirmed as real. Truth reflects reality.

The truth is that you are probably a better human than you realize. The truth is that your weaknesses don't have to be your undoing. But the truth is also that you'd probably like to have some of your past choices back and would love not to repeat them. The truth is that you are unconditionally loved by God and there's nothing you can do about it.

It may be difficult to believe that such things are true. So don't pray to believe these things. Pray to see them as living realities. Then the truth will be undeniable.

> *Jesus said, "If you hold to my teaching, you are really my disciples. Then you will know the truth, and the truth will set you free."*
> *—John 8:31–32*

Who Is True?

Unless you've been there, it probably makes no difference to you whether it's true that Paris, France, exists.

You probably learned about its existence in school. You've seen pictures; perhaps you've watched movies or read books about it. If someone handed you a plane ticket, you'd probably get on board with the belief that what you've always heard is true: that Paris, France, exists. But just because it's true that something exists, what difference does it make?

Now consider the most faithful person you've ever known. She is someone on whom you can depend. When she says she'll be somewhere, she shows up. When she tells you something, you can take it to the bank. When she makes you a promise, she keeps it. She doesn't just speak the truth. She is true.

Truth matters. But who is *true to you* matters even more.

Without faith it is impossible to please God, because anyone who comes to him must believe that he exists and that he rewards those who earnestly seek him. —Hebrews 11:6

Life Outside the Cave

Feeling the arms of your spouse around you after a fight. You and your friends laughing hysterically over a cup of coffee. Seeing an unexpected check come in the mail to help pay the bills. Taking time off work to chaperone your kid at summer youth camp. Spending the day accomplishing so much that you forgot to eat.

This is life outside the cave. It's not as simple or familiar as the shadows of the superficial life. It will require more of you and challenge you in ways you can't imagine. But it is the life that matters, the life that is real and true, the life that has meaning.

And you're going to need some assistance living out here among the real, so you'll need to get as close as you can to the source of life outside the cave . . . by raising your eyes to the Son above.

Jesus . . . said, "I am the light of the world. Whoever follows me will never walk in darkness, but will have the light of life."
—John 8:12

What Is Beyond You

It was the world of your childhood.

The street on which you lived wasn't a street; it was a frontier to be explored. The house two blocks down was the subject of rumor and unsettling stories. The woods nearby were full of strange creatures and thrilling unknowns. You strained your neck to stare at grown-ups, and they seemed large enough to burst beyond the frame of your vision.

Most everything you saw in the world was beyond you, which was both a fearful and wonderful thing.

Then you grew up and were told that being an adult means having all the answers, understanding everything you see, and managing all your responsibilities and relationships with precision. Knowing in your heart that such a life is impossible, you retreated into the safety of the superficial.

But your childhood heart understood it: the life that matters is beyond any of us.

Return to your sense of wonder.

"Truly I tell you, unless you change and become like little children, you will never enter the kingdom of heaven." —Matthew 18:3

Beyond Understanding

Much of what matters is discovered when we wrestle with mystery, the areas of life beyond our understanding.

The character of the human spirit is certainly a mystery. Women are mysterious to men, as men are to women. Teenagers are in their own category of mystery to the average parent. Humans are complex, simple, and full of unpredictable emotion.

And then the even deeper mysteries: If God exists, why won't He prove His existence? If God is loving, how can He allow evil and suffering? What happens after you die?

Understanding is important. There are answers out there for many of your questions. But it is in negotiating mystery that you're forced to move beyond yourself into the realm of faith and trust.

So the ultimate question perhaps isn't, "What do you know?"

It is, "Whom do you trust?"

Oh, the depth of the riches of the wisdom and knowledge of God!
How unsearchable his judgments, and his paths beyond tracing
out. . . . For from him and through him and for him are all things.
—Romans 11:33, 36

Beyond What Is Seen

There was a monster under the bed. You couldn't see it, but you knew. Under the bed, in the closet—it was always what you couldn't see that scared you most.

But the unseen also thrilled you. Imagining what lay outside your door every day made you tie your shoelaces all the quicker. Imagining what gifts were yours under the Christmas tree filled you with anticipation and joy.

As adults, we're still scared of the unseen, all those areas beyond our control. And we've also lost that sense of wonder about what's outside our door or the gifts waiting to be opened.

But God will turn on the night light and leave the door cracked. And He'll invite you to discover a world of wonder that only He can reveal.

Will you trust this God of the unseen?

Now faith is confidence in what we hope for and assurance about what we do not see. . . . By faith we understand that the universe was formed at God's command, so that what is seen was not made out of what was visible. —Hebrews 11:1, 3

Beyond What's Expected

Do surprise parties ever work anymore?

You plan, you demand secrecy, you park all the cars down the street, everyone hides, and you yell, "Surprise!" The person smiles, laughs, and acts like he can't believe this is happening but later reveals that he suspected it all along.

We've lost the wonder of surprise. In fact, as much as we can, we order our lives so that we face nothing unexpected. We wake up at the same time. We work the same job or stay in the same field for years. We pay the same bills. We see the same people. Go to the same places. Think the same thoughts. Over and over and over.

When was the last time you were truly astonished? Bowled over by surprise? Don't be afraid to step out of your comfort zone, shake things up, and expect the unexpected.

"What no eye has seen, what no ear has heard, and what no human mind has conceived"—the things God has prepared for those who love him—these are the things God has revealed to us by his Spirit. —1 Corinthians 2:9–10

Beyond What's Possible

The people who planned crowd control at the big theme parks are geniuses.

For some rides, you can spend an hour or more in line. People often wait in sweltering heat, whining kids in tow, but somehow they stay relatively content.

One reason is the design of the line itself. You're surrounded by walls and can only see about twenty feet in front of you. Then you turn a corner and face yet another twenty feet. You don't know what's around each corner, so each time you're hopeful that around the next bend, you'll reach your destination.

Most challenges we face are full of segmented turns. We could never imagine accomplishing that task, overcoming this trial, but we turn the bend and it's only another twenty feet. And after that, who knows?

Is what you see all that there is? Is what's possible *all* that is possible?

Trust the One who designed the theme park.

If the blind put their hand in God's, they find their way more surely than those who see but have not faith or purpose. —Helen Keller

Prayer

Prayer is putting wonder into words.

What is it that you need? Speak to the One who supplies every need. What are you straining to understand? Trust the One who will reveal it to you. What fears have you tied in knots? Lift them to the heavens and remember He's bigger than any monster under the bed. Thank Him for how He has made the impossible possible, and ask Him for courage when you round the next turn.

Sometimes, what's beyond you feels so overwhelming that you have no words. It's all you can do to drop to your knees and just ask to feel His presence. To know that this God of wonders comes near when we pray and meets our every need.

Maybe not in the way we expect. Maybe not on the timetable we'd like. But He is there all the same.

The Spirit helps us in our weakness. We do not know what we ought to pray for, but the Spirit himself intercedes for us through wordless groans. —Romans 8:26

Beyond Life Itself

One of the chief wonders of childhood is that you feel as though you'll live forever.

You tackle life with abandon. You have an energy to learn, to enjoy, and to discover that would leave the most elite athlete in the dust. Your wonder for life sustains you because as far as you're concerned, life has no end.

And then you grow up and learn about retirement plans and life insurance. You still build and plan a life, but it has an expiration date, and so your world is limited by a span of years. If there *is* any magic to be found, it will —like you—eventually fade away and die.

It's true. We will all die someday. But will that be the end of life? Or is there more life to be lived?

Your answer to that question will determine whether you'll start running again with joyful abandon.

"I am the resurrection and the life. The one who believes in me will live, even though they die; and whoever lives by believing in me will never die. Do you believe this?" —John 11:25–26

Creation

In most cultures, it's believed that in order to truly see the world and your place in it, you have to know where you come from. Usually, this is limited to tracing your family history. But you also need to understand the God who created you in the first place.

God, like any artist or inventor, has a vested, intimate interest in His creation, so much so that He was present in creation from the beginning.

We look at life and so often find ourselves alone—despondent, hopeless, and empty—not unlike the vain and formless chaos in the first verses of Genesis. But if you look again, you'll see you are connected to a Creator who is both present and much closer than you think.

That should radically change the way you see the world.

"[God] marked out their appointed times in history . . . so that they would seek him and perhaps reach out for him and find him, though he is not far from any one of us. 'For in him we live and move and have our being.'" —Acts 17:26–28

Nature

There's an experience in nature, standing before a mountain range or at the edge of an ocean, where you encounter something so beautiful that you're left in complete awe. You're overwhelmed, but also fully alive. And your focus can find no other object to behold.

Have you ever seen nature this way? If not, realize that cathedrals for worship can be found as close as the nearest park or forest trail. The Creator's signature can be found in every blade of grass, the chirping call of spring's first birds, the unseen wind as it washes over your face.

Like God, nature's size and force should fill you with a sense of amazement while energizing you with its living power.

Want to have a better view for what matters? Fall in love with nature.

The heavens declare the glory of God; the skies proclaim the work of his hands. —Psalm 19:1

Beauty

As a joke, some artists have drawn up what the Barbie doll might look like at age fifty: hair with tints of gray, baggy eyes, and a decidedly thicker frame. But still with that blissful, smiling stare.

It represents many more women than the young blonde ever could. It also reminds us that our culture often has an odd standard for what's considered beautiful.

True beauty is most often appreciated through connection. Husbands still look adoringly at their wives in old age. Parents always see the beauty in their children. You are God's child, and He'll always find you beautiful.

When connected to your Creator, you'll see more and more of the beauty in everything. The beauty of creation echoes back in thanksgiving for what God has made it to be.

Ask the earth and the sea, the plains and the mountains, the sky and the clouds, the stars and the sun, the fish and the animals, and all of them will say, 'We are beautiful because God made us.' This beauty is their testimony to God. —Augustine of Hippo

Imagination

Hollywood has nothing on the imagination of God. Visit the zoo or watch a few nature documentaries. You'll be tickled by the outrageous palette of color in birds and fish. The design and shape in the platypus and aardvark defy the efforts of the best special effects guy on the most expensive movie set.

In creation there is a serene order, a feast for the senses that bewilders as much as it inspires. It reminds us that too often our best ideas are merely pencil-drawn stick men compared to the infinite imagination of our Creator.

Creation should inspire your imagination. But your job isn't so much to create something out of nothing or come up with that one original idea. Your job, as one of God's creatures, is simply to reflect the imagination of the One who made you.

Do that, and the sky's the limit on what you can imagine and do.

Now to him who is able to do immeasurably more than all we ask
or imagine, according to his power that is at work within us.
—Ephesians 3:20

Inspiration

Have you ever gone sailing? The wind blows, and the boat moves. The sail and other mechanisms will affect the boat's direction, and a sailor can use the wind to set his desired course. But should there be no wind, or too much, the boat is the victim of nature's whims.

Like most creatures, you're made alive by the winds and breath of creation. And you're kept alive by the very breath that you breathe. You're inspired to be who you were created to be by the breath and Spirit of God.

God spoke with a mighty breath and the world was created. God still speaks and reminds us that we're alive and still have work to do. And, despite our occasional success in controlling the winds of life, we must rely on His inspiration to move in the direction He would take us.

The Lord God formed a man from the dust of the ground and breathed into his nostrils the breath of life, and the man became a living being. —Genesis 2:7

Stewardship

It's hard to recognize how the created world connects us to God, to stand in awe of its mountains and oceans, to celebrate its beauty, to be moved by its breath of inspiration—and not want to protect this temple of worship for ourselves and future generations.

Some say it's silly to imagine that we could have any real impact on nature. Some point out that God gave us creation for our benefit. All this is true to a degree. But any gift should be handled with care and respect. It should be honored because it bears the mark of the Divine.

So while recognizing nature's power and benefiting from its resources, we can certainly take steps to leave it like we found it.

In stewarding creation, we honor its Chief Architect to whom we owe our life and being.

The LORD God took the man and put him in the Garden of Eden to work it and take care of it. —Genesis 2:15

What Is Glorious

I hope you've been up early enough to witness a sunrise. Certainly you've seen a sunset as the afternoon has faded into dusk.

Sunrise and sunset—a brushstroked mingling of color and radiance that stops you in your tracks and reminds you that your earthly thoughts are trivial—and that there's more to the world than your senses have ever imagined.

Like the sunrise and the sunset, when you reflect your connection to your Creator in what you say and do, you shine back a heavenly prism of light that declares His glory for all to see.

His glory in the skies and in the reflections of your heart are a reminder that none of us are alone. We've been touched by the Divine and have been created to live for Him.

Do not be afraid, for I am with you; I will bring your children from the east and gather you from the west. . . . Everyone who is called by my name, whom I created for my glory, whom I formed and made. —Isaiah 43:5, 7

Art

Art shows us the beauty of both God and man. As created beings, we're an extension of His creative works. So how we create on His behalf goes far beyond works of art, though works of art are still one of the best ways to encourage that creative impulse.

Just as you relate to nature, you can connect to the Divine through art, but the encounter is sometimes more striking because it also reminds you of your connection to other human beings. In enjoying the works of an author or a painter, you're joining them in community as they explore that connection.

By raising your awareness of art, you're daring to imagine the works of art *you* might create. Perhaps on the page or the blank canvas, but more importantly, in your creative contribution to life itself.

> *He has filled them with skill to do all kinds of work . . . all of them skilled workers and designers. —Exodus 35:35*

Books

Books are perhaps the most personal of all art forms. They can delve deeper into the inner pockets of your psyche than other mediums.

You were probably read to as a child. Curled up on your mother's lap, you remember her soft tone as she acted out the story with the rise and fall of her voice. You looked at all the pictures and were allowed to turn the pages.

You can probably still recall books from your youth. They were friends who understood you, who invited you to journey with them on some fantastic adventure. There was a warmth and safety as your eyes crossed the printed page.

Even today, you might use books to regroup, to make some sense of the chaos, and to spur you on toward greater things.

Books can reach inside our minds and give us a sense of ownership in understanding the life that matters.

Everywhere I have sought rest and not found it, except sitting in a corner by myself with a little book. —Thomas à Kempis

Music

The average person has never attended an opera, but here's why you should try it at least once. At first, it may feel frustrating. Most operas are sung in other languages, so you may find yourself focusing on the subtitles to make sense of the story.

But then you learn something: you can better follow the story by simply immersing yourself in the music. It's in the music where you'll best encounter the drama playing out before you.

Music engages the parts of your soul for which there are no words. Where books infuse the mind, music ignites the emotions. If not opera, it could be a catchy pop song or a stirring rendition of the national anthem.

Music reminds us that our story isn't just meant to be seen, but heard. And not just heard, but felt. Music reminds us that the life that matters is meant to be felt as much as understood.

Next to the Word of God, the noble art of music is the greatest treasure in the world. It controls our thoughts, minds, hearts, and spirits. —Martin Luther

Movies

The theater goes dark. The twenty minutes of previews are finally over. The world around you changes as you are transported into an entirely different realm.

You are a bird in flight soaring over mountains. You are frozen by the sorrow of a character you've grown to love in a matter of minutes. You double over in belly laughter over comedic antics you'd never try at home. You're stirred by the broken love of a couple trying to find their way.

Movies are perhaps the closest we can get in art to learning by example. They combine what's best in most other art forms—words, music, and visuals—to show us pictures that move. They transport our mind and emotions outside the mundane and the ordinary into territory we might just explore for ourselves one day.

The best movies can be a model for living—or at least entertaining—the life that matters.

Where I was born and where and how I have lived is unimportant. It is what I have done with where I have been that should be of interest. —Dwight L. Moody

Art That Matters

Art is often meant to simply entertain. It can soothe our frazzled nerves. It can help us escape the pressures of our day.

However, as you take inventory of your life and consider how better to live for what matters, you'll want to take a look at your artistic "diet." How much of the entertainment that you consume is junk food and how much actually enriches your soul?

It's not always about being a puritan when it comes to content, or about throwing out all your silly comedies for PBS documentaries. It's about eating a balanced diet.

In many books, music, movies, plays, and paintings, the artist's chief goal is to inspire us to wrestle with and ponder the life that matters. These can be spiritual works; works that teach us something we didn't know about the human condition; works that educate; works that elevate; works that remind us that we're meant to be creators too.

The highest art is always the most religious, and the greatest artist is always a devout person. —Abraham Lincoln

You, the Artist

Everyone should be an artist.

You could write a blog for friends or you could publish a book. You could learn how to paint landscapes or you could decorate your home. You could join a choir or sing Christmas carols in nursing homes. You could learn how to create beautiful pottery or restore a classic automobile.

Part of developing yourself as a person who matters is to explore how to express yourself artistically.

You'll soon discover what you have a passion and talent for and what you don't. But even in the areas where it's clear you don't have a strong talent, it's still important to at least try different art forms. These will stretch your vision for how to see the world creatively and how to live creatively.

Don't worry. It's part of who you are. Pick up your pen, clean your paintbrush, warm up your vocals, and get started.

Ready. Set. Create.

On the walls all around the temple, in both the inner and outer
rooms, he carved cherubim, palm trees and open flowers.
—1 Kings 6:29

What You Create

In the movie *Mr. Holland's Opus*, Glen Holland is a high school music director who, for thirty years, had dreams of composing music. But instead, he taught children who were often rebellious and unappreciative of the power of music.

On his last day, he's shocked to discover an auditorium full of students who've gathered to pay him tribute. They tell him that his creative contribution wasn't just about composing music, but about composing a future for students who needed his creative input to succeed. The students themselves, he is told, are the notes of his "opus," or symphony.

You're here to create works of art. Some may be books or songs. Most will be displayed in people who've benefited from your talent to help create in them the life that matters.

God is creating that life in you. What will you create in others?

In the beginning God created the heavens and the earth. —Genesis 1:1

The Productivity of Others

If you're like many, your eyes may start to glaze over a bit when you hear the latest economic report. The Dow is up or down. Imports are exceeding exports. Interest rates are holding steady in the third quarter.

Yawn. For most, such facts fail to capture our interest. They have meaning and importance, but what's the average person supposed to do about it? The problem this creates is the belief that you actually have nothing to do with the success of industry. But you do.

As previously mentioned, your productivity matters. But so does the productivity, or industry, of others. Especially the productivity of the community that surrounds you. And that's where your main focus should be. Not necessarily on the national or global level, but in the five to ten miles surrounding your local neighborhood.

This is where superficial consumerism evolves into organic community. You should be intentional about supporting the productivity of others.

I am a success today because I had a friend who believed in me and I didn't have the heart to let him down. —Abraham Lincoln

Mom-and-Pop

They're up very early. They were probably up late the night before, poring over receipts and various accounts. They turn on the lights and make sure everything is clean and in order. They check supplies, welcome sleepy employees, and rotate the window sign from Closed to Open.

And then they wait, praying, *I hope we have a good day.*

We are a materialistic culture, and we often buy stuff we just don't need. But while thrift and simplicity do matter, so does contributing to the financial security and sense of purpose of your neighbor.

In supporting your local mom-and-pop establishments, you aren't just buying stuff; you're supporting families, people who want to stand on their own two feet, people who are hoping this dream they've pursued won't fail.

Inside those store windows are people who matter. And buying from them is a gift.

[They] must work, doing something useful with their own hands,
that they may have something to share with those in need.
—*Ephesians 4:28*

Near to the Source

They're up even earlier.

Milking cows, feeding livestock, harvesting crops, traveling to town on a Saturday morning to set up their booth at the local market, praying, *I hope we have a good day*.

We wander through the produce or meat section and rarely imagine where our food comes from. But if the farms throughout our country were to suddenly disappear, we'd quickly notice the difference.

What farmers produce is near and dear to the source of what matters. And like the mom-and-pop stores, they're just trying to keep that dream alive, one more season, one more year.

And while there's nothing wrong with buying your goods at the larger stores, try to direct more and more of your purchases to your neighborhood farmer—at the local farmers market, meat market, or co-op.

They haven't come all the way into town for nothing.

The hardworking farmer should be the first to receive a share of the crops. —2 Timothy 2:6

Handmade Joy

You'll also find arts and crafts at your local market or county fair: baskets, glassware, woodworking, furniture, pottery, jewelry, handmade clothing, embroidery, scrapbook supplies, paintings, and so on.

A quilt maker was once asked why she toiled through the hours and painstaking attention to detail required to produce a quilt. Was it for the money? "No," said the quilter. "I do it for love."

Many crafts such as marriage quilts, beaded jewelry, knitted items, and custom wood cabinets are made for love. They're meant to be passed down from one generation to the next as family heirlooms.

Others may be sold in your local market or antique shop, but they too are handmade labors of love. To buy a basket or a piece of pottery is to receive a gift that matters—the fruit of someone's creative passion.

The special joy of another person enters your home, and that joy is passed on to you.

The Christian shoemaker does his duty not by putting little crosses on the shoes, but by making good shoes, because God is interested in good craftsmanship. —Martin Luther

Fair Trade

For Sale: Washer and dryer. Gently used. *Well, maybe not gently, but lovingly used. Okay, used several times a day for five years washing soiled kids' clothes over and over (and over), my husband's boxer shorts (did I just say that?), sometimes items like car keys, action figures, and pocket change. It runs okay. We'll sell it cheap. I'm just desperately in need of a new one. Will you help? Please?*

You probably wouldn't see many ads like this in your local paper or online classifieds. But if you filtered classified ads through a lie detector, they just might start to look a little more like this!

Buying used goods from individuals or at yard sales is a way to help others live a life that matters. You're helping them purge items they don't need, make extra income, and improve the efficiency of their home. You're also saving yourself money in the process.

Consider how you can support your neighbor in the realm of fair trade.

And don't forget to haggle.

If you make a sale, moreover, to your friend or buy from your friend's hand, you shall not wrong one another.
—Leviticus 25:14 *NASB*

Buy the Lemonade

If you haven't bought lemonade from a seven-year-old recently, shame on you.

He makes the sign. His mother helps him stir in the mixture and set up the table. And when the first neighbor walks up and puts a dollar in the jar, you'd think that kid had won the lottery!

A tingle of excitement comes when we realize that something we do can actually earn us money. For a kid, it might be pocket change for candy. For an adult, it's paying the electric bill and buying groceries. It means having a sense of pride and a purpose for living.

Supporting the employment of others shouldn't just be left to business owners or government agencies. See a sign for a guy who'll mow your lawn? Call him. Find an ad for a local handyman? Give him a try. Have a skill or trade you can teach? Go down to your nearest community center and teach it.

When you put that dollar in the seven-year-old's jar, you'll be purchasing a lot more than lemonade.

The poor man with industry is happier than the rich man in idleness. —Henry Ward Beecher

Backward and Forward

Bigger isn't always better.

Can sprawling strip malls, new fast-food joints, and big box stores improve the local economy? Sure.

But when such progress results in local farmers losing contracts to the corporate big dogs, when mom-and-pops have to close their stores because they can't compete, when the life of your community moves from the cozy downtown storefront to the rectangular concrete out on the state highway, maybe progress isn't really progress after all.

Sometimes to move forward, you need to take a step back. Maybe the best way to move your community forward is to preserve what was good about it in the first place.

Most people who work on farms, who run their own businesses, who sell what they've made with their own hands, are working for more than just money. They're working toward a life that matters.

The more you're aware of and can contribute to that kind of industry, the further along you'll be.

You can settle among us; the land is open to you. Live in it, trade in it, and acquire property in it. —Genesis 34:10

Surrounded by Time

Why does your awareness of time matter?

Because time is about context. And context defines you.

Context is what surrounds, and what surrounds tends to define you and provide meaning to what you think, say, and do. For instance, the word *trunk*, while spelled exactly the same, is defined differently when surrounded by phrases like "a hickory trunk in the forest," "a swaying trunk in the African jungle," or "a padlocked trunk in the baggage compartment."

You are surrounded by your past, present, and future. Who you are, what you think, and what you do will most often be guided by what time it is.

Too often—when we lose track of time, the season we're in, how we fit into what has come before, and where we're going—we lose our bearings for how to be, how to think, and what we should be doing.

What time is it where you are? It matters.

You may delay, but time will not. —Benjamin Franklin

Good Morning

Every day has a genesis.

The sun rises, the world awakens, and you remember the hope you had just twenty-four hours before. It's a new day. Again!

Yesterday was a disaster. You made a monumental mistake. You made someone so angry, you were sure she was done with you. You felt so depressed that you could barely breathe.

But that day is behind you. Time marches on. And often, that's a good thing.

You failed? Pick yourself up and get back on the horse. You made progress on some goal? It's time to make even more progress. You went to bed exhausted? The night's sleep has refilled your tank for today's challenges.

Morning is the time when who you are isn't so bad, your thoughts can be renewed, and what you do is full of hope and expectation.

Don't be alarmed by the clock when you wake—it's time to begin again.

In the morning, Lord, you hear my voice; in the morning I lay my requests before you and wait expectantly. —Psalm 5:3

The Season You're In

People often struggle to appreciate the season they're in. In the heat of summer, they dream of snow. In the cold gray of January, they dream of barbecues and swimming pools. And although many favor the moderate seasons of spring and fall, too often those times are also marked with an impatience for what's next.

In the same way that spring can be linked with renewal, summer with vitality, fall with letting go, and winter with death, so too do the seasons you're living through have similar themes. And it's important that you don't miss what they have to teach you.

What time is it for you? Is it a time to start over, a time to embrace life's fullness? Is it a time to regroup and let go, or a time for closure and moving on?

Here's something to remember about seasons: they have a purpose. And they're temporary.

Don't miss the season you're in.

There is a time for everything, and a season for every activity under the heavens. —Ecclesiastes 3:1

A Student of History

Has a scent or song ever taken you back to a long-forgotten event from years past? Our senses can provide such triggers.

What does that tell you? For one, it says that your brain is a vast database of historical knowledge, and also that much of that history is hidden inside without your awareness.

We're told that it's important to be students of history. Reviewing past events involving nations, social movements, and famous individuals is said to help inform who we are in the present and who we may become in the future.

You can't change your history, but you should become its student. There may lie hidden in your psyche significant or even traumatic events that affect who you are today, memories that can solve the mystery of why you do the things you do.

The past is past. But it may be time to stop and see what has made you who you are.

Dwell in the past and you'll lose an eye. Forget the past and you'll lose both eyes. —Russian proverb

Your Time Is Now

The mayfly seems like a tragic creature.

Mayflies are insects that develop in a water environment, from which, after a growth period lasting around a year, they finally emerge as adults in a form not unlike a butterfly.

They then take flight above the water, find a mate, lay eggs . . . and they die—after only one day.

When polled on what they would do with only one day to live, people's responses varied. Some would over-indulge in pleasure or tell off their boss. Some would spend time with loved ones and ask for forgiveness from those they've hurt.

While you could have fifty more years, none of us is guaranteed our next breath. What would you do with that time?

Perhaps the mayfly's life *isn't* so tragic. Maybe it chooses to fly, to love, to leave behind a legacy, because it knows its time is now.

There's no tragedy in time well-spent.

Dost thou love life? Then do not squander time, for that's the stuff life is made of. —Benjamin Franklin

What's Ahead

Living just for today can be taken to extremes. You've heard of groups expecting the world to end any day. Many stock up on food and supplies. Some hide out in the mountains. Some even end their lives.

While recognizing that your life *could* end at any moment, you also need to plan as if you had fifty years to live. You need to live for today, but also for what's ahead.

Planning for the future matters because your life isn't meant to be only a series of small, ad-libbed moments. You're also here for the great moments—finishing your education, launching your children into adulthood, celebrating decades of marriage, finally achieving a sense of contentedness and peace that had so long eluded you.

None of this happens overnight. And none of this happens without seeing a future that's both possible and worth pursuing.

Commit to the Lord whatever you do, and he will establish your plans. —Proverbs 16:3

As Day Fades into Night

You've had a long day.

You look back on all you did. The impacts you made, the mistakes, the laughter, the love.

You sit on your porch swing and watch as the day fades into night. The fireflies dance. The crickets serenade. It feels right to sit here and notice that time is short. And that it is all okay.

At the end of your day, or at the end of your life, imagine yourself looking back with a sense of peace. You didn't waste your time. You welcomed new beginnings, you enjoyed each season, you didn't allow history to repeat itself, you lived for today, you planned for tomorrow.

You defined your life by the time you were in. You lived for the One who lives outside of time.

The clock winds down, slumber beckons, and the darkness of night turns into the light of forever.

From everlasting to everlasting you are God. . . . A thousand years in your sight are like a day that has just gone by, or like a watch in the night. Yet you sweep people away in the sleep of death.
—*Psalm 90:2, 4–5*

PART 3:

HOW TO FREE YOURSELF FROM THE RAT RACE

You Need Your Rest

Roller coasters are a fun ride. They thrill you with their twists and turns. They terrify you with the illusion that you're in mortal peril. They exhaust you with the relentless ups and downs.

But imagine that you couldn't get off the roller coaster. You had no break from enduring it over and over, without pause. Then it wouldn't be nearly as enjoyable.

Too many of us choose to stay on the roller coaster. We work too many hours. When we're not working, it's home projects, family obligations, committee meetings, or church events. We never lay off the gas pedal and wonder why we have nothing left in the tank.

Your body, mind, and spirit—and the world itself—run on a cycle of work and rest. It's not just about ceasing activity, it's about refreshment and restoration.

It's time to get off the roller coaster. You need your rest.

When I surveyed all that my hands had done and what I had toiled to achieve, everything was meaningless, a chasing after the wind; nothing was gained under the sun. —Ecclesiastes 2:11

One Day in Seven

You're home from work, but it's not time to sit down. Laundry. Dinner. Dishes. Putting the kids to bed. Will it never end?

You're working your tail off on the job, but the boss wants the project completed next week. Sure it's Sunday, but it has to be done.

Part of freeing yourself from the rat race is realizing that if you follow the work-rest cycles God has set in place, He'll often restore the time you didn't think you had, or He'll reveal that your tasks weren't as urgent as you thought.

God also wants to see if you'll stop working and trust that He's the real breadwinner. That's a big reason why worship is set aside for one day in seven. It's both an act of faith and an act of reverence for your ultimate Provider.

So if your work seems never ending, rest anyway. It will restore your soul.

My soul finds rest in God; my salvation comes from him. Truly he is my rock and my salvation; he is my fortress, I will never be shaken.
—Psalm 62:1–2

Getting Away from It All

Let's face it. Most vacations are hardly restful.

You spend hours in the car with cranky family members or you arrive at the airport to find that your flight's been delayed. You pay extraordinary prices for lodging, food, and mementos; if visiting family, you sleep on a bed too small for you and bicker with relatives about which restaurant to go to.

You return home exhausted, thinking you could sure use a vacation.

In order to rest, you need to get away from it all. And while the rare vacation might suffice, you need it far more often than once a year. If possible, you should do it every day; you need time away from everything. Everything that steals energy from your body, mind, and spirit.

So while sleep is certainly one way to restore your body, you also need a vacation for your mind and spirit.

But Jesus often withdrew to lonely places and prayed. —Luke 5:16

A Fast for the Senses

No TV. No music. No smartphone or tablet. No children. No husband. No wife. No friends. No talking. Close your eyes. What do you hear?

Silence.

At first, you'll feel uncomfortable. Okay, you'll feel more than uncomfortable—it may actually feel a bit terrifying. But your mind and your spirit need a break. Relax. You'll realize you don't need all that noise.

You can hear a few things. Shutting out the world like this actually allows you to remember they are there.

Your breathing, for one. It's one of the most important things you do that you never acknowledge. Take several deep, slow breaths. It's almost like hearing yourself live. If you're outside . . . birds, lawn mowers, kids playing down the street. Listen for the wind. That's almost like hearing the world live.

Sleeping restores your body. Resting your senses while awake restores your soul.

Let him sit alone in silence, for the LORD has laid it on him.
—Lamentations 3:28

Deep Thoughts

Once you've purged your mind of the noise, you can start to fill it again.

But slowly. Methodically. Deeply.

Find a good book. The Bible is a good book. Other books can serve this purpose too. It should be a book about what matters. A book that can hit you right between the eyes with just one line. It should speak to the deepest parts of you. It should stir. Inspire. It should give you a foundation to engage the chaos.

Keep silent as you read. Remember to breathe. Remember to listen.

Take notes. What's coming to the surface as you read?

Pray about what you read, write, and think. Lift your thoughts to God and ask Him what He thinks.

Remember: rest isn't just about the absence of activity. It's about freeing your mind and spirit so that they might be built up again.

Think deeply.

Whatsoever things are true, whatsoever things are honest, whatsoever things are just, whatsoever things are pure, whatsoever things are lovely, whatsoever things are of good report . . . think on these things. —Philippians 4:8 KJV

Slowing Down

In the early 1980s, Steven Newman set out from Bethel, Ohio, and proceeded to walk around the world. That's right. He spent four years and walked 15,509 miles around the world. He lived to tell the tale in his book, *WorldWalk*.

Steven's pace had to be slow, of course. So as he walked, he was able to notice everything. The warped shape of corn stalks in a farmer's field. Chipped paint on old houses. A line of ants marching to battle on the side of the road.

And he noticed people too. Many invited him into their homes, where he ate meals with them and learned about who they were. The kindness of people around the world was one of his greatest discoveries.

Too often, we speed by life at eighty miles per hour. And we miss it. There is so much to see. To enjoy and to love.

We don't need to walk around the world to discover it. We just need to slow down. And rest in what we see.

I'm a slow walker, but I never walk back. —Abraham Lincoln

Refreshment

You haven't slept this long in ages. And boy, did you need it. It didn't seem possible. You were so tired. You had absolutely nothing left. Your thoughts, emotions— completely drained. But now your eyes are clear. You have new energy. Your brain is welcoming new thoughts. The day seems possible again. You feel refreshed.

The world has a rhythm. Just like your breath. It breathes out. It breathes in. It exhausts its energy. It restores. It begins again.

It's one thing to march to the beat of your own drum. It's another to always fight against the rhythms of rest and refreshment God has created for you to enjoy. If you want the fuel to enjoy the life that matters, you need to stop and listen for that beat.

"Come to me, all you who are weary and burdened, and I will give you rest. Take my yoke upon you and learn from me, for I am gentle and humble in heart, and you will find rest for your souls. For my yoke is easy and my burden is light." —Matthew 11:28–30

Serenity Now

Reinhold Niebuhr's *Serenity Prayer* has been used by Alcoholics Anonymous and other recovery groups for decades.

And for good reason.

People in recovery admit that their lives are no longer manageable. They have sought peace from the chaos through substance abuse, but that has left their lives in even more devastation. They realize that true peace comes only from accepting what's out of their control, and in taking responsibility for what's in their control.

No one can function long without a sense of peace or security. If your life is in constant conflict—with yourself, with others—you'll never be able to move beyond self-interest to embrace what matters. You'll hide in the safety of superficial living. Or worse, you'll medicate with substances like alcohol.

You don't need to be in AA to admit that life often feels unmanageable. If God is your higher power, ask for serenity now.

God, grant me the serenity to accept the things I cannot change,
the courage to change the things I can, and the wisdom to know the
difference. —Reinhold Niebuhr

A False Peace

Prime Minister of England in the late 1930s, Neville Chamberlain was a leader who wished to preserve peace at all costs.

And while this would be wise under most political scenarios, with the aggressive evil of Adolf Hitler on the loose, many argue that it was the wrong course of action. It is said that Chamberlain's appeasement allowed Hitler to rise to power and start World War II.

Our goal should always be one of peace. But by avoiding conflict that already exists in our lives, we can, like Chamberlain, sometimes create a false sense of peace that can lead to even greater suffering.

What areas of trouble or conflict do you sweep under the rug, hoping they will just go away? Are you living in a false sense of peace? It won't last. And it will likely lead to greater suffering.

Your troubles need to be faced if you're ever to find true peace.

They dress the wound of my people as though it were not serious.
"Peace, peace," they say, when there is no peace. —Jeremiah 6:14

Peace Through Surrender

Here's a simple definition of war:

War is a conflict where the strengths and weaknesses of each side are exposed so that one side eventually conquers, and the other side surrenders, resulting in peace.

The wars you face will expose your weaknesses. They will give you the opportunity to accept the things you cannot change, and if you choose to see it, they will expose God's strength and the need to surrender to His strength.

Surrendering is scary. But know that God is more than just some distant higher power. He is someone who loves you deeply. He's someone who will stand faithful when you're ready to give up. He will hold your troubles in safekeeping and offer you a peace that passes understanding.

Will you surrender your troubles to Him?

Do not be anxious about anything, but in every situation, by prayer and petition, with thanksgiving, present your requests to God. And the peace of God, which transcends all understanding, will guard your hearts and your minds in Christ Jesus. —Philippians 4:6–7

Peace with Yourself

The war has raged inside you far too long.

Two opponents fighting it out over and over, leaving the landscape of your soul in shambles: the battle between *what you say you want* versus *how you actually live*.

Perhaps your battle is between wanting to stay clean and a track record for relapse. Or wanting to love your husband, but constantly tearing him down. Perhaps it's as simple as wanting to face the pressures of daily life, but never finding the strength.

Admit it. The war inside has broken you. But once you learn to surrender to God, your healing will begin. Only God can reconcile what you say you want with how you live. Through His peace, you can have peace with yourself.

And be whole again.

There is now no condemnation for those who are in Christ Jesus, because through Christ Jesus the law of the Spirit who gives life has set you free from the law of sin and death. . . . The mind governed by the flesh is death, but the mind governed by the Spirit is life and peace. —Romans 8:1–2, 6

Peace with Others

They looked so happy. I can't believe they're getting a divorce.

Have you ever heard this? A couple is married, sometimes for decades, and it seems like the perfect marriage. And then, without notice, it ends. What happened?

Many marriages that look perfectly peaceful still end in divorce. Very often, the couple lived in a false peace and never sought to work through the conflict that lay beneath the surface.

One thing builds on another. Peace with God. Peace with yourself. Peace with others.

A marriage, or any relationship, will only prosper if the two parties see conflict as an opportunity to admit their weaknesses, to surrender to God, and to allow Him to make them whole.

Only people who are in the process of being made whole will have the strength to love another person over the long term despite their weaknesses.

To fight for unity and peace.

Be completely humble and gentle; be patient, bearing with one another in love. Make every effort to keep the unity of the Spirit through the bond of peace. —Ephesians 4:2–3

The God Who Is in Control

Children have very little power.

They are frail. They need protection. They're often afraid of the unknown.

When it comes to our troubles, we're often no different than a child. We like to think we can handle every obstacle, but we just can't. Understanding this is a path to true, lasting peace.

As much as you're a helpless child, God is the loving parent you may have never had. When you come inside crying over a scraped knee, He doesn't lecture you to be more careful. He instead lifts you up on His knee like a tender Father. He wipes away your tears, kisses your forehead, and tells you it's all going to be okay.

Use the anxiety that suffocates your spirit as an opportunity to climb into the lap of the One who will hold you and keep you safe.

The God who is in control over all that lies beyond your grasp.

I have calmed and quieted myself, I am like a weaned child with its mother; like a weaned child I am content. —Psalm 131:2

Just for Today

A phrase is added to the Serenity Prayer in many recovery group meetings: *just for today*. It's actually a variation on the longer version of Niebuhr's prayer: "living one day at a time, enjoying one moment at a time."

You don't have to be addicted to alcohol or drugs for life to feel unmanageable. Facing your problems, surrendering, finding peace within yourself, working for peace with others, and giving control to God are the keys to peace. But none of this happens overnight, so even if you're pursuing these strategies, you can still find yourself overwhelmed.

God has a job and you have a job. Your main job is to focus on the peace of today—very often, on peace in the next moment.

Have the wisdom to know that tomorrow will worry about itself. The time for your peace and serenity is *now*.

"Therefore do not worry about tomorrow, for tomorrow will worry about itself. Each day has enough trouble of its own."
—Matthew 6:34

The Single-Wide Life

In the late 1990s, Rich Mullins was a successful recording artist and millionaire.

But you'd never know it.

He asked his accountants to never tell him his income. Instead, he wanted to receive the salary of the average working man. The rest went to charity.

Rich lived in a single-wide trailer on a remote Navajo reservation in Arizona. And when he wasn't touring, he spent his days teaching Native American children about the beauty of music.

From the standards of the world, Rich had everything. But he chose to give up everything in order to live in the abundance of the life that matters.

Most of us are not wise or disciplined enough to sift through the distractions of excess—whether it's too much money, too large a home, or piles of stuff cluttering our senses.

So while you may not have the courage of Rich Mullins, consider that you may need to turn the American Dream on its head to pursue the life of simplicity.

For our boast is this, the testimony of our conscience, that we behaved in the world with simplicity and godly sincerity.
—*2 Corinthians 1:12 ESV*

Cooked by Small Degrees

You've heard about the frog in the pot of water? It's said if you place a frog in a pot of boiling water, he'll jump right out. However, if you place him in cold water and increase its temperature by small degrees, the frog won't notice and will eventually find himself cooked.

Clutter is like this. No one would live in a house full of clutter. But you place a piece of junk mail on your desk, buy another pair of shoes, bring home a chair from the yard sale. Six months goes by and your house looks like the city dump. Your frog has been cooked!

Whether it's paper, clothes, or furniture, most of us are lucky if we can manage what's right in front of us, not to mention a life full of too much stuff.

You'll never be at home with what matters if your home is too full of the stuff that doesn't.

Whoever loves money never has enough; whoever loves wealth is never satisfied with their income. —Ecclesiastes 5:10

Stockholm Syndrome

Where do you start?

Most of the time, it's with one pile, one closet, or one box at a time. It entered your home that way; it can leave that way.

Really, it'd be easier to send it all to the local dump, but your emotions won't allow you to make such a bold move. It's almost like the real-world example of the Stockholm syndrome. You're held captive. Suffocating. But you also have an attachment to your captor. It's a mess, but it's *your* mess. It feels safe.

It is a type of hostage negotiation, but essentially, you're negotiating with yourself. Keep. Toss. Purge. Have someone help you if you can't talk yourself down. And if negotiations fail, you'll have to be ruthless. No matter how it feels, this stuff is not your friend.

The purge will be painful. It will feel impossible.

But it has to be done.

Use it up, wear it out, make it do, or do without.
—household proverb

Guarding Your Space

Your house is clean.

It's like living in a congested city and then spending the weekend in the mountains. You had no idea exactly how repressive the clutter was until you were free of it.

But how do you not let it happen again?

It's really a reversal of how you likely got rid of it in the first place. You probably had to make tough choices on what you really needed, or how often it would actually be used. If it didn't qualify, out it went! You need to use the same scrutiny now when considering what, if anything, should enter your home again.

The simplicity of space and what material objects should demand your focus is something that needs to be protected. Remember: you got yourself into this mess one choice at a time. You can guard your space exactly the same way.

"Be on your guard against all kinds of greed; life does not consist in an abundance of possessions." —Luke 12:15

The Fragmented Life

It's not just what's in your house.

We also can make our *lives* too complicated. We juggle too many projects. We overcommit to clubs or church or kids' activities. Or due to social pressure, we divide our persona between who we are in front of others and who we are in private.

The work it takes to manage such a fragmented life wears us to the bone.

In the same way you purged your stuff, then, you may need to purge the activities or people that just don't matter. Do your kids really need to be involved in so many activities? Do you? Are some of your friends so caught up in their own baggage that they barely know you exist?

Like your house, once your life is clean of these activities and people, you'll wonder why they ever mattered to you in the first place.

Jesus looked at him and loved him. "One thing you lack," he said. "Go, sell everything you have and give to the poor, and you will have treasure in heaven. Then come, follow me." —Mark 10:21

Simplicity Has a Number

Simplicity has a number.

One.

The real goal of simplicity isn't just about minimizing what pulls your focus to only a few things. It's also about teaching you how to focus on one thing at a time.

We are so distracted. One of the chief virtues in our society is being a multitasker, but few of us are really able to pull that one off effectively. Simplicity reminds us that quality matters more than quantity. The less we have to manage, the more devotion we'll give to it.

Simplicity will purify your heart so you can walk better by faith. To see that among all the gadgets, activities, and people that occupy your life, you truly only need one thing.

God himself.

Simplicity is really about a devotion and singleness of vision to realize that the unseen source of all you see is really all you need.

Whom have I in heaven but you? And earth has nothing I desire besides you. —Psalm 73:25

The Pursuit of Happiness

Rich Mullins had finally made it.

After slaving away in Nashville as a songwriter and recording artist, he had some number-one hits. His studio told him he could finally write his own ticket! Headlining his own tour, millions in income, a new house, new car, the works. He'd achieved the American Dream.

And he told them no thanks. He left Nashville, went back to college, and then moved to an Arizona single-wide to live his dream of simplicity.

In 1997, Rich was tragically killed in an automobile accident. He was part of the rat race, but escaped to pursue the happiness that only comes through a singular devotion to God and to the least of these.

Simplicity is a gift. But it's a gift that's only received when we choose to give away what the world thinks matters.

Do you want what *truly* matters? Then give the rest away.

"For whoever wants to save their life will lose it, but whoever loses their life for me will find it." —Matthew 16:25

Trusting in the Provision of God

What is it that truly brings joy and happiness?

Some might say winning the lottery. Win the lottery and you no longer have to worry. You'd have all the money you need and life would be good.

But you've heard the stories. Many who win are not happy. Some end up in bankruptcy. Many lose family and friends. Some even die.

Why? Perhaps it's because once they finally have so much, they're in constant fear of losing it. Or once they have the power to buy whatever they want, they realize they can't buy what they really need.

Some people say that money is the root of all evil. But it's not money. It's the *love* of money. In order to get free from the rat race, you simply need to learn how to put money in its place. The role money should really play is to remind you that money doesn't matter.

Trusting in God as your provider is what matters.

For the love of money is a root of all kinds of evil. —1 Timothy 6:10

The Numbers Don't Lie

Budgeting. It's not a four-letter word, but it might as well be. You have to learn how to budget. And once you learn, it takes time to manage. But that's not the biggest reason most of us avoid budgeting.

It's because the numbers don't lie.

Budgeting shows us what we care most about, and too often it's not the stuff that matters. But after the sting of that admission fades, it can be an important step to righting the ship again.

Do your spending patterns point to a desire for instant gratification? Budgeting can help you learn to trust in God enough to wait for what you want, or to show you what you don't really need.

The discipline of budgeting can also help you take responsibility for what God has provided you to live on, and it can help rein in other areas in your life as well.

The numbers are telling you the truth. It's time to spend what you have to fund the life that matters.

Keep your lives free from the love of money and be content with what you have, because God has said, "Never will I leave you; never will I forsake you." —Hebrews 13:5

Stop the Bleeding

Perhaps the numbers have left you hopeless.

The balances you owe on your credit cards could fund a small country. You send your money in so many directions that you couldn't imagine what to address first. What's the point of even trying?

But say you cut your arm and started bleeding profusely. You wouldn't waste your time being glum about your plight or fret about how the cut could possibly heal one day—you'd tie some cloth around your arm to stop the bleeding.

So maybe the first admission about your finances needs to be that you have a bad cut that needs immediate attention. You may not feel like you're dying, but if you're buried under the consequences of unwise spending, you're certainly not living.

Putting a stopper on unnecessary spending may feel as tight as a tourniquet, but it's what has to happen first if you're ever going to heal.

Some people, eager for money, have wandered from the faith and pierced themselves with many griefs. —1 Timothy 6:10

To Be Poor in Spirit

We're not just talking about money here.

Money is just a mechanism to describe who you are and what you care about. It doesn't truly meet your needs in the way we imagine. God does.

Of course, God isn't standing there ordering the cashier to place groceries in your bag. They want money. The point is that God is the source of all there is. Mountains. Buildings. People. Governments. Economies. Money.

Not everyone is poor. Some people in this world without money are suffering, but everyone is poor in spirit, whether they realize it or not. Everyone needs God. And how you handle your money is often an indication of whether you're aware of this truth.

If your need for God and your trust in His provision drives how you earn your money and how you spend it, you will find your fortune, no matter how much is in your bank account.

"Blessed are the poor in spirit, for theirs is the kingdom of heaven."
—Matthew 5:3

Investing in the Future

Part of the reason it's good to get your finances under control is so that you can start investing.

Investing means placing your money or resources into some venture, expecting that it will eventually return a profit. With a savings account, you'll earn interest, but mainly the saved money will profit you down the road when you most need it. Some invest in retirement, stocks, or businesses.

But you can also invest your time in the life of another person. You can invest yourself in learning, in healing, in living the life that matters.

And that's the point. It's more than just money. Does God want you to earn enough to put food on the table? Of course. But ultimately God wants you to go beyond living paycheck to paycheck.

He wants you to invest in a future that matters.

"Store up for yourselves treasures in heaven, where moths and vermin do not destroy, and where thieves do not break in and steal. For where your treasure is, there your heart will be also."
—Matthew 6:20—21

Giving Away What Was Never Yours

The Source of all things is also the Owner of all things. There's a pleasure in giving what you have to someone in need that is unlike the pleasure of ownership. You place your money in the Salvation Amy tin. You volunteer to serve dinner to the homeless. You see the look in a poor child's eyes when you hand them a box covered in colorful Christmas wrapping.

But your whole life is actually a gift. God gave you life and you are His. God so loved that He gave. Whether it's your money, your talents, or your time, the more you walk in gratitude for what's been given to you and the more you realize that what you have was never really yours in the first place, the more you'll offer everything you have to those in need.

God has provided you with the means to give. And it's in the giving that you'll receive.

Give generously to them and do so without a grudging heart; then because of this the LORD your God will bless you in all your work and in everything you put your hand to. —Deuteronomy 15:10

Prosperity

Are you rich in faith? Do you put your trust in the God of the unseen?

If you do, or if you're learning to do so, or even if you want to do so, you can be prosperous in all that you do.

The test money provides is whether you want to just live in the prosperity of material fulfillment or in the richness of relationship with your Creator. He is faithful to provide you with what you need, but what you ultimately need is God Himself.

You evaluate your spending, you budget, you don't panic when you're poor, you invest, you give it all away. Not because you should, not because it's yours, but because you're *His*. And because He takes care of His own.

The fact is that you've already won the lottery. Not by chance, but by eternal purpose.

What will you do with this newfound treasure?

So Abraham called that place The Lord Will Provide. And to this day it is said, "On the mountain of the Lord it will be provided."
—Genesis 22:14

Beachfront Property

Have you ever caught a newscast of hurricane devastation in places like Florida and then heard a few years later that all the beachfront property has been rebuilt? Why build a structure that is likely to be destroyed over and over by the elements?

Yet that's how many of us live our lives. We settle in unstable environments and wonder why our lives are so often in ruins.

Have any instability in your world? Relationships? Work? Home life?

If you don't have stability, you have no chance of building a life with any integrity or staying power. You'll always live in fear of the next storm. You'll never have the security required to focus on the healing and growth we all need to prosper.

If you want to build a life that matters, it may be time to get off the beach and look for safer territory.

"But everyone who hears these words of mine and does not put them into practice is like a foolish man who built his house on sand."
—Matthew 7:26

Drama Junkies

It sure seems like some people remain on the beach because they like a good hurricane. You spot them on the newscasts, running around in those 90-mile-per-hour winds. What are they thinking?

But some lives just aren't working unless they're in the midst of drama. People stay in abusive relationships. Coworkers move from one office scandal to the next. Some people are always sick or in financial trouble. Some families need their own reality show.

Of course, not everyone invites drama, but others have never really known a life without it. They grew up that way. Their parents lived it. They either don't know how to get free of it, or don't think they deserve to be free.

If that's you, please know that a stable life is out there. You are not destined to endure one hurricane after another.

If you bite and devour each other, watch out or you will be destroyed by each other. —Galatians 5:15

How Firm Is Your Foundation?

Of course, moving off the beach won't save you from storms. They'll still come. So once you find safer territory, how you build matters. And strength starts with building a good foundation.

That's essentially the point of this book. Is your life founded on what matters? Have you placed your roots in a strong sense of identity? Of purpose? Are you connected to your Creator and grounded in reality? The higher you want to rise in life, the deeper and more stable your foundation should be.

God is often referred to as a rock. A rock you can cling to amid the strongest winds. A rock that has never faltered. Solid. Faithful. Firm.

Why not build your life on Him?

"Everyone who hears these words of mine and puts them into practice is like a wise man who built his house on the rock. The rain came down, the streams rose, and the winds blew and beat against that house; yet it did not fall, because it had its foundation on the rock." —Matthew 7:24–25

Brick and Mortar

Away from beaches and hurricanes, the heartland can still experience severe storms. Tornadoes, although less widespread than oceanic storms, can have even more destructive power if you take a direct hit.

That's one reason why folks don't recommend you live in a mobile home. In fact, when a tornado warning goes off, it's said that it's better for you to lie in a ditch than to assume that your mobile home will protect you. Even if the mobile home rests on a decent foundation, the walls and internal structure are like papîer-maché against the strongest storms.

You've left the hurricane alley; you've chosen a strong foundation. If you're going to rebuild, stable building materials are vital. Really, some good brick and mortar—material as close as you can find to the rock of your foundation—would be wisest.

Just as you received Christ Jesus as Lord, continue to live your lives in him, rooted and built up in him, strengthened in the faith as you were taught, and overflowing with thankfulness.
—Colossians 2:6–7

Social Security

Once you've made the decision to create more stability for yourself, it's important to make good choices about what types of people you rebuild your life with.

Remember, you're no longer a drama junkie. You can avoid those who are still stuck in that addiction.

We're not talking about expecting perfect people. But it's good to find those who are also building on a firm foundation, whose general structure is sound, preferably people who live in a classic brownstone, who've weathered decades of storms and have lived to tell about it.

Perhaps the only thing better than a sturdy house is a strong and secure neighborhood. You check on your neighbors when they're sick. You look out for each other in good times and bad. You're not afraid to walk your dog after dark. It's a safe place to grow, raise your kids, to have a life.

Surround yourself with stable people. They matter.

Bad company corrupts good character. —1 Corinthians 15:33

Deeds of Trust

Here's something else to look for in choosing your neighbors.

Stable people are dependable. When they say they'll be somewhere, they show up. When they make you a promise, they keep it. Maybe not all the time, but most of the time.

But their integrity doesn't necessarily lie in a good upbringing or some freakish strength no one else could match. Many stable people have simply learned to put their trust in the God who is faithful and have learned to become more trustworthy as a result.

And, that's the beauty of a good neighbor. They tend to rub off on you. When you've never known much stability, or are having trouble finding strength in this unseen God, you can trust in the deeds of those God has already strengthened.

Perhaps there will be a day when they'll need your strength too. That's how it works.

A friend loves at all times, and a brother is born for a time of adversity. —Proverbs 17:17

Walking on Water

It's wise to move off the beach, to head inland, to build on a solid foundation, to use brick and mortar, to choose dependable neighbors.

Despite this, the storms will still come. Destructive winds will blow. Flood waters will rise and even the strongest house will eventually feel the strain.

But here's some great news. Living the life that matters isn't just about being stable enough to weather the storms. It's about embracing a God who looks into the eye of the hurricane and says, "Peace, be still." It's about looking to the God who is at rest in the strongest storm. His foundation is so strong that He can even walk on the stormy waters.

And when He invites you to come, you too can walk atop those raging waves as if they were solid ground.

Jesus went out to them, walking on the lake. . . . "Lord, if it's you," Peter replied, "tell me to come to you on the water." "Come," he said. Then Peter got down out of the boat, walked on the water and came toward Jesus. —Matthew 14:25, 28–29

When Everything Is Personal

Here's the problem: much of the rat race really has nothing to do with us.

We turn on the national news and hear about the latest conflict overseas. Or the stock market rising or falling. Or Congress arguing over this or that bill. We hear that another celebrity is back in rehab. We obsess over the dysfunctions of people we've never met.

Certain national or global issues shouldn't be ignored, and there are those who are called to address them. But most of us aren't. We could probably make more of a difference calling our local city councilman than we can by wringing our hands over the latest national debate.

It's when you take *everything* personally, including issues that have no immediate bearing on your daily life, that you can lose track of what matters.

It's probably time to make your world a great deal smaller and see what you might be missing.

I neglect God and his angels for the noise of a fly, for the rattling of a coach, for the whining of a door. —John Donne

Firsthand Accounts

When's the last time you received a hand-written note? Personal words of appreciation, where someone took the time to write about how highly they think of you, perhaps sharing something from their life?

When's the last time you had a face-to-face, lengthy conversation with another person? A warm exchange of personal news or discussion about a struggle you were going through?

Such exchanges are rare these days. We don't get our news in notes or personal conversation. We spend our time enticed by gossip, juicy details that mean more to us than learning a firsthand account of someone's story.

And very often our focus is on the news of some celebrity or national figure, usually untrue and always far removed from the world playing out right in front of our eyes.

What's new? Shut off the computer or TV. Pick up some stationary or meet someone for coffee, and find out for yourself.

[Don't give] up meeting together, as some are in the habit of doing, but encouraging one another. —Hebrews 10:25

The World Just Down the Street

Sometimes the best way to escape the rat race is to just get out of the house.

Spending too much time obsessed with the well-being of TV characters you've never met? *Real people* just down the road are meeting in support groups, Bible studies, bowling leagues, and craft clubs.

Always complaining about how much suffering there is in the world? Volunteer at a church or community center. Stock market got you down? Join a local trade group. Washington politics occupying your brain? Attend some city council meetings or run for office yourself.

Life is about balance. Sometimes you need the peace and quiet of home. But if you're constantly preoccupied with issues that are miles beyond your grasp, you're still running the rat race from the comfort of your couch.

Either stop worrying about this stuff altogether, or get out there and do something about it. The world just down the street is what most deserves your attention.

I alone cannot change the world, but I can cast a stone across the waters to create many ripples. —Mother Teresa

What Is Routine

Normality gets a bad rap. If life is to be exciting, it's said, you need to embrace change! You have to shake up the apple cart and welcome the chaos!

While it is important to challenge yourself and not stay stuck in a rut, you probably face plenty of change and chaos without ever having to seek it out. So you also need to protect, as much as possible, a life filled with, dare we say it?

Routine.

Children need routine. People with emotional and mental disabilities can't live without it. Most adults need it too. The natural world has the occasional upheaval—earthquakes, storms—but most of the time, it runs itself by predictable routines. Every day the sun rises and sets. Every year, the seasons change.

We depend on these cycles. And if you're looking with the right eyes, you'll grow to love them.

Those who work their land will have abundant food, but those who chase fantasies have no sense. —Proverbs 12:11

Seeing What's Familiar

Your first night in a hotel room is exciting. The nice big bed, the large TV, the tiny bottles of shampoo. But the second night, it feels more stale, almost empty. It has no life. Usually it's because, other than your personal items, it has nothing that's familiar.

Soldiers cope mentally and emotionally by carrying something familiar with them. Photos of loved ones, the latest letter from home. When we're far away from what we know, we need to hold on to familiar anchors.

But even if you return home every day and see your loved ones, it's easy to get so stressed out by the rat race that you ignore the very touchstones that can bring you back to your senses.

No matter where you are or what you are dealing with, never lose sight of what's familiar. It will sustain you and fill your tank when you're feeling adrift from what matters.

I thank my God every time I remember you. . . . It is right for me to feel this way about all of you, since I have you in my heart.
—Philippians 1:3, 7

Protecting What's Personal

What's personal will sustain you when the rat race seems the most frenzied. The rat race will try to rob you of what's personal. It will tempt you to put more "urgent" priorities above what really matters.

So what's personal needs protecting. You're going to need to stand up to the chaos and set some boundaries so it can't get in.

Have a weekly phone call with your parents? Let nothing get in the way of that. Your kid has a baseball game Saturday? Tell your calendar that this is a non-negotiable. Too tired to go to tonight's support group? Tough. Sometimes you even need to set boundaries for yourself.

The rat race doesn't care about what matters. You need to care enough about what matters to not allow the rats to win.

Let your eyes look straight ahead; fix your gaze directly before you.
—Proverbs 4:25

Home

You and your spouse are just waking up. You talk. You smile. You share intimacies reserved for no one else.

The kids are playing in your backyard. They run and bounce with an endless energy. Their laughter seems to intermingle with the soft clouds and sunlight.

You're in your dining room with close friends for dinner. You rave about the food. You share stories. You tell silly jokes. The house is full of friendship.

Home. What's on the wall, the furniture, the people, even the mess—it's yours. It's where you can be you. Home is where life is most personal.

You're in your private room. You tell God what you can tell no one else. You ask for His guidance. You feel His presence and His comfort.

Home is wherever the cares of the world have no hold.

Jesus [said], "Anyone who loves me will obey my teaching. My Father will love them, and we will come to them and make our home with them." —John 14:23

Uncool Is the New Cool

We're always the mice racing after the newest cheese. The latest fashions. The newest gadget or software release. The newest fad diet. But typically the very moment you grab the new thing, it becomes obsolete. The cheese has changed and it's time to get back in the race.

What are we really chasing? A way to look cool? If we are honest, most of us are not cool and never will be. More likely, we're hungering to belong. We race after what's cool in an endless desire for acceptance.

If you're pursuing what matters, cool will usually be the last thing on your mind because what matters is nothing new. It's been around for thousands of years, so most often the last place you'll find it is in what's cool. Usually it's in what's outdated, what's traditional, what's nice, or what's considered nerdy.

What's truly cool is belonging to what matters.

All these people were still living by faith when they died . . .
admitting that they were foreigners and strangers on earth.
—*Hebrews 11:13*

Lessons in Nostalgia

If you want to get a taste for what matters, knock on the door of an elderly lady and ask her to tell you her story.

She'll weave her tale with a mixture of joy and melancholy, often referring to objects in the house as props for her history lesson: an ornate cabinet that was her immigrant grandmother's. An old mirror given to her before she met her husband. A push-pedal pump organ she first played on as a child. She'll direct you to family portraits captured from long ago.

And you'll leave richer than when you came in.

This woman, her mementos, and her memories remind us that the world has been running long before we ever arrived on the scene. Connecting to what has come before is usually our best bet for grounding ourselves in what matters.

Whether it folks with some history, traditions, or ancient ideas, what the culture of cool considers useless and outdated is often far more useful for discovering what we most need to learn.

[L]et the wise listen and add to their learning, and let the discerning get guidance. —Proverbs 1:5

The Strength of Tradition

In the early 1950s, approximately one-third of the Indiana State Police force was engaged in a standoff with some normally harmless farmers in Onward, Indiana. In the name of progress, the state had ordered Onward's high school to disband and be consolidated with nearby Walton.

But for a town like theirs, the high school, and particularly the traditional Friday night basketball game, was the lifeblood of the community. They were not going to give it up without a fight.

Through a series of negotiations, the police eventually backed down. Against the mighty forces of the new and improved, this little town defended what was theirs.

Traditions of community and belief go back to the very beginning of history. Their strength is in the connection between one generation and the next. Not every tradition is rooted in what matters, but many are.

If you find yourself confronted by forces of superficial progress, seek out and defend traditions worth keeping.

Progress means getting nearer to the place you want to be. And if you have taken a wrong turning, then to go forward does not get you any nearer. —C. S. Lewis

The Heights of Mediocrity

The world of cool is obsessed with reaching the top of the mountain.

Our movies are full of superheroes and secret agents. We worship the success of celebrities and athletes. We care more about who is going to win *American Idol* than we do about someone stepping out to sing his or her first church solo on a Sunday morning.

It's not that we shouldn't dream big. But living the mountaintop life most often has little to do with how many people we reach or whether our story would be big enough for the news.

Consider the story of Jesus. God came from the highest of heavenly heights to reach people at the lowest and most common levels. He most often made a mountaintop impact on people in ways that would be rejected by today's gatekeepers of success.

So what may seem mediocre to the culture of cool is—according to God's model—at the highest heights in the life that matters.

The art of being happy lies in the power of extracting happiness from common things. —Henry Ward Beecher

Release Your Inner Nice

The Lawrence Welk Show was a program featuring big band music and other traditional fare. The costumes and hairstyles now seem comical. The melodies, the dancing—it all seems terribly corny compared to the TV of today.

Today the culture of cool is entertained by the grit and grime of the "real world": illicit sex, graphic violence, backstabbing, vindictive selfishness.

Old shows like *Lawrence Welk* are just nice. And while *nice* might feel like too simple a word, it reminds us that there is more to us than our animal instincts. There is a purity and brightness of spirit worth celebrating too.

The behavior we see in today's media does exist, but if that's our main focus, we'll be cool in a world without hope, a world that has abandoned any possibility that *nice* could ever exist again.

You can still catch *Lawrence Welk* on TV. Turn it on sometime. Have a laugh at its hokey packaging. And release your inner nice.

Like newborn babies, crave pure spiritual milk, so that by it you may grow up in your salvation. —1 Peter 2:2

Nerds for Christ

The nerd culture is alive and well and living in America. These folks attend sci-fi and comic book conventions. They spend hours online discussing their favorite show or video game. They celebrate all things *nerd*.

It's not just that these people share a passion for creative storytelling. It's that, having never fit in with the world of cool, joining forces with other nerds gives them a sense of belonging.

Followers of Jesus Christ are no different really. We're people who admit we don't quite fit in, and we join in community with others who feel the same way. Our leader stood up against the culture of cool so that we could finally belong.

Perhaps you're one of us. You'll never be cool in the eyes of the world, but you can belong to the life that matters.

You are no longer foreigners and strangers, but fellow citizens with God's people and also members of his household. —Ephesians 2:19

Belonging to What Matters

Think about some people who have made a real impact on our world: Mother Teresa, Martin Luther King Jr., Mahatma Gandhi, Jesus Christ.

They probably weren't the most popular in school. Their fashion choices have never graced a magazine cover. They weren't beautiful according to the world's standards. Really, according to the culture of cool, we shouldn't give them a second glance.

But they reminded people of the importance of connecting to what has come before. They defended traditions worth preserving. They showed that heaven exists among the lowly and common and that we can become better people.

Mostly, they shared a message of love and belonging, that there is more to life than fitting in and looking cool.

What you've been looking for in the new and improved has been here all along. You can take a rest from the race and belong to a people and a life that matters.

Do not conform to the pattern of this world, but be transformed by the renewing of your mind. —Romans 12:2

Choosing Joy

The world is a weary place.

The news reports murder and violence. Children are abused. Nations war. Our personal lives are messy. Dysfunctional families. Loveless marriages. It too often seems that there's little in life to celebrate.

So when someone tells us to be more joyful, we feel that to force a smile amid all this pain would mean donning a mask we're just too tired to wear.

But consider this: despite all the darkness, there is still light in the world. And the mere existence of darkness doesn't disqualify the power of the light.

Choosing joy is a discipline. But it's not about faking it or manipulating your emotions. It's about training your eyes to see the light in the darkness and to regularly celebrate what you see.

There is a time to take life seriously. But there's also a time to rest from the race, to let down your guard, and to rejoice in the life you've been given.

This is the day that the LORD has made; let us rejoice and be glad in it.
—Psalm 118:24 ESV

Mining for Diamonds

Choosing joy is like mining for diamonds. No matter how dark it is, you can find precious jewels if only you'll dig a little.

List your gratitudes. You're alive; you're loved; you can love others. Most likely, you have a roof over your head and food on the table. And that's just a start. Remembering your gratitudes is the key to joy.

See the light right in front of you. There's rarely a moment where you can't find some glimpses of light wherever you are.

Imagine what makes you joyful. Time with your sweetheart, your children, your pets, chocolate cake, a large pizza, sleeping in, waterskiing, you name it.

Sing a joyful song. Your favorite pop tune, a church hymn, a song from your childhood. Try it. It works!

There's no denying the darkness within the mine. It's how you spend your time down here that will determine your joy.

The light shines in the darkness, and the darkness has not overcome it. —John 1:5 ESV

Laughter

Norman Cousins suffered from an illness that often left him in searing pain. However, he discovered a natural way to address it.

He realized that laughter releases endorphins, a natural painkiller and pleasure inducer, and that as little as ten minutes of strong belly laughter could give him as much as two hours of pain-free sleep.

It is said that laughter is the result of a collision between what we expect and what we don't. Outrageous behavior, uncomfortable situations, a joke that sends us in one direction and, with a punch line, sends us reeling in another direction.

Laughter is a natural response to what seems outrageous or impossible. And isn't that often what you face in daily life?

The very challenges and absurdities you face are often no different than some ridiculous comedy sketch. Laughter is simply a way to release yourself from the burden of mastering life's absurdities.

So have a good laugh. Like Norman Cousins, you may find freedom from the pain.

A cheerful heart is good medicine, but a crushed spirit dries up the bones. —Proverbs 17:22

Duck Duck Goose

If you ever need a refill on your joy meter, play Duck Duck Goose with a few five-year-olds.

A picker walks around a circle of children, touching one head at a time, saying, "Duck, duck . . ." Eventually the picker taps a head and says, "Goose!" and the goose chases the picker around the circle, trying to tag him or her. You can imagine how silly and crazed it can get. If you ever join in as an adult, you'll remember what silliness feels like.

Children have a knack for this unconditional, rapturous silliness—unrestrained belly laughs, melodious giggles, bursting enthusiasm, playful absorption.

As often as possible, try taking off your adult hat and returning to the land of silliness, where worry has no place and life has no limits, where the only task to be completed is embracing life to its fullest.

Although you can never return to childhood, you *can* join children in play and learn from these masters of joy.

He will yet fill your mouth with laughter and your lips with shouts of joy. —Job 8:21

Make Time to Play

Spend some time with children and you'll remember that play is the fuel for life. Working adults need the release of recreation and play perhaps more than any child.

But if you are a working adult, your life is full of competing responsibilities. So ironically, you'll likely need to schedule your play and make it part of your routine. Recreation matters just as much as eating, sleeping, and paying the bills.

Plan weekend trips or summer vacations at state parks, the beach, or the mountains. Visit museums and browse antique shops. Take up walking, jogging, or bike riding, or join an amateur sports team. Arrange regular game nights with family or friends. Join a book club. Try out different restaurants. Go out for live music. Join a choir, orchestra, or community theater.

Your joy is limited only by your lack of imagination. Make time to play.

The real joy of life is in its play. . . . [It] is the business of childhood, and its continuation in later years is the prolongation of youth.
—*Walter Rauschenbusch*

Breaking Bread

The table is large. You look around and see almost everyone you love. You can barely see the polished wood surface for all the bowls and platters of homemade food. You start to fill your plate. You pass to the left. Your belly and your heart are filled to the brim.

You smell burning charcoal mixing with the summer breeze. The grill master is hovering over the grill, ready to flip burgers at a moment's notice. You can barely see the picnic table for all the potato salad, beans, and sweet tea. You share quiet conversation and laughter with your favorite people. There can be no better day than today.

If you're like most people, two of your favorite things are probably eating and spending time with family and friends. Part of living the joyful life is combining those two as often as possible.

The joy of food and fellowship is meant to be savored. Eat it up. Drink it in. And come back for more.

Every day they continued to meet together. . . . They broke bread in their homes and ate together with glad and sincere hearts.
—Acts 2:46

Pleasures Forevermore

Life is meant to be enjoyed. And the key to enjoying life's pleasures is to make God your chief pleasure.

God loves you unconditionally. Do you take pleasure in that? God will never quit on you. He'll never leave you. God has a plan for you. Doesn't that fill you with joy?

God wants to meet your every need and has given you all He has in the gift of His Son. God is just waiting to show you His mercy. He wants to release you from your hopelessness and shame. God has a life for you beyond what you currently see. How can you not be bursting with joy?

But here's the best news: if God commands you to be joyful no matter how you feel, then He *will* fill you with joy once you choose to obey.

The light shines in the darkness. It shines on pleasures that will never end.

You will show me the path of life; In Your presence is fullness of joy;
At Your right hand are pleasures forevermore. —Psalm 16:11 *NKJV*

Living Above and Beyond

Here's something you probably don't know about rats: their only real interest is survival.

Rats scurry. They run from place to place in fear of predators (and probably other rats). When they're not in fear, they only know their hunger. Their only thought is the next piece of cheese.

You will never escape the rat race unless you realize you're not a rat.

Unlike rats and other animals, you were made in the image of a heavenly Creator, so you must see your life as more than just about surviving from day to day, running in fear, and only focusing on that next piece of cheese.

God offers you a life that certainly includes the things of earth, but He also offers you life above and beyond. But you don't have to wait for eternity to experience this. Life at its fullest, both earthly and heavenly, can begin the moment you determine to live for more.

"The thief comes only to steal and kill and destroy; I have come that they may have life, and have it to the full." —John 10:10

Living Courageously

If you've ever listened to an interview for a soldier awarded for courage under fire, you often hear a fact that seems contradictory to the citation: the soldier was afraid.

Most soldiers who have seen combat will admit this, but we've bought the myth that the soldier who fights courageously has no fear.

It's not that they weren't afraid, they'll say. It's that something was more important than their fear—love of country, pride in their cause, the lives of fellow soldiers. Their courage was essentially a value judgment that the things that matter are more important than letting fear run their lives.

Does fear run your life? It's okay to be afraid. But you'll never live above and beyond if you're frozen in place or prone to retreat. If you don't believe what matters is more important than what scares you, you'll never put fear in its place and charge forward to take the next hill.

For God has not given us a spirit of fear, but of power and of love and of a sound mind. —2 Timothy 1:7 NKJV

Living for What Energizes

Energetic people may inspire you, or they may drive you nuts. This usually depends on where their energy comes from.

Are they an exposed bit of electric wire, driven by the tyranny of the urgent? These people are exhausting. They want you to buy into their frenzy, and if you don't, they resent you and move on to someone else.

Or are they folks charged by the spark of what matters? With these, you may find a similar bounciness, but there's a warmth and generosity to their fire. If they invite you to join them, it's more about sharing in their joy or giving you a taste for what feeds their soul.

You want to be around people with that kind of energy. It's more refreshing than exhausting, more freeing than full of obligation. It can help free you from the rat race while giving you supernatural fuel to run for the life that matters.

We should all be thankful for those people who rekindle the inner spirit. —Albert Schweitzer

Living for What Enriches

We'd prefer not to think about it, but rats don't eat just cheese.

Really, rats are scavengers and will eat just about anything they can find, no matter how disgusting. This is probably why they have such a low reputation in the animal kingdom.

Perhaps you've found that when you're always on the go, run ragged by your own race, you tend to eat poorly. You spend more time in the drive-through lane. Your freezer is full of processed food. Made from scratch, home-cooked meals are few and far between.

Likewise, when your life is one big rat race, you also can play the scavenger. You get your "nutrients" wherever you can find them. Fast-food entertainment, canned information, processed inspiration.

You are what you eat. When it comes to feeding your soul, don't compromise on your diet. Live for what enriches.

This will bring health to your body and nourishment to your bones.
—Proverbs 3:8

Living for What Is Noble

British period dramas provide a few lessons in living above and beyond.

Women wear demure gowns and whisper about handsome suitors and modest virtues. The men—donned in tails and ruffles—stand as ready protectors of king and country. It's a bit elitist to be sure, but there is also an admirable quality to this royal standard of decorum.

As a child in God's kingdom, you will find yourself raised to the status of nobility. So as you stand up a bit straighter, wearing your Sunday best, you too can rise to this standard—in what you think, what you say, and in the honor and respect you hold for others.

You don't have to look like a snob. More likely, you'll have the grateful look of one who knows you were snatched from the rat-infested streets to stand at court in the palace of the King.

You are a chosen people, a royal priesthood, a holy nation, God's special possession, that you may declare the praises of him who called you out of darkness into his wonderful light. —1 Peter 2:9

Living for the Impossible

Did you ever stop to think that what we consider a miracle is not so supernatural to God? As the Creator of all things possible, He simply arranges the chess pieces in the created order to advance His purposes.

Too often, we settle only for what's possible, but what we're really settling for is what *we* think is possible. We're created beings, not the Creator Himself.

So the issue returns to one of trust or belief. If you're constantly stuck in the rat race, your first admission should probably be that you don't believe it's possible to escape it at all. What will you trust in, then? Your own view of what's possible or the God who makes all things possible?

And if you believe that God can free you from the rat race, then what else might be possible? This is the God who created everything out of nothing and who brings the dead back to life.

Are the limitations in your world too hard for someone like Him?

"All things are possible to him who believes." —Mark 9:23 NKJV

Dying to Live

Do you want to live life to the fullest? Do you want to *really* live?

Then you need to be willing to die for it.

You first have to die to your need to just survive. You have to kill off the fear that paralyzes and live for what's new and challenging. You have to pronounce dead the tyranny of the urgent and live for joy and refreshment. You have to trade the superficial for what enriches, your pauper status for nobility, and the possible for the impossible.

The death you have to die isn't a meaningless death. It's a death that leads to life above and beyond the life you've imagined.

The God who offers you life at its fullest died so you could live. Die to the idea that you are just a rat in a race, and choose to live above and beyond for Him.

"Whoever wants to save their life will lose it, but whoever loses their life for me and for the gospel will save it." —Mark 8:35

PART 4:

THE IMPORTANCE OF YOUR RELATIONSHIPS

Life Is Relationship

Do you know when God first noticed something was wrong with the world He'd created? It wasn't Eve and the apple. It was Adam, standing by himself in the garden. In the face of His glorious creation, God saw that something was still incomplete. He said, "It is not good that man should be alone."

And still today, we all feel this in our deepest heart. As the cliché goes, *no one on their deathbed ever wished they spent more time at the office.* When you look back over your life, what will ultimately matter will be your personal relationships. Your family. Your spouse. Your children. Your closest friends.

If life matters at all, it's in loving and being loved. But it's not a guarantee. It's an opportunity, and it becomes something like a gift.

Life is relationship. It is not good for you to be alone.

The Lord God said, "It is not good for the man to be alone. I will make a helper suitable for him." —Genesis 2:18

The Source of All Relationship

Here's some fine print. As meaningful as our human relationships are, they often fail us, and we're left searching for something more.

So ask yourself this question: If you agree that what makes life worth living are your personal relationships, then wouldn't the source of life also be personal and relational? If God is the source of all relationship, then perhaps the source is purer than what's downstream.

Even when all your human relationships fail you, God can be the father, sister, mother, brother, or even the loved one you may have never had. As you get to know this loving God, you can also see your human relationships more infused with the integrity and love you always wanted from them.

If God is the source, maybe that's where you should start in making all your relationships matter.

We know and rely on the love God has for us. God is love. Whoever lives in love lives in God, and God in them. —1 John 4:16

The Story of Relationship

God is the source of all relationship. He created the world for relationship. And so the story of the Bible is also the story of relationship.

The pages of Scripture speak of a God who desires to be present and intimate with you and to speak to you in your loneliness. He says such things as, "Do not be afraid, for I am with you," and, "I will . . . walk among you and be your God, and you shall be my people."

And all the other dynamics of relationship—the tenderness of a nurturing mother, the discipline of a protective father, the wonder of childhood, the sanctity of marriage, the pain of betrayal, the comfort of a friend during grief, the safety of family—these all can be found in the story of God's relationship to man.

Who doesn't like a good story? It's His story. And it's yours too.

To fall in love with God is the greatest of all romances; to seek Him, the greatest adventure; to find him, the greatest human achievement. —Augustine of Hippo

The Beginning of Relationship

Every relationship has a beginning. The butterflies fluttering in your stomach on a first date. Shaking hands with someone new and wondering if you'll be friends. Holding your baby in your arms for the very first time.

The beginning of all relationship happened when God formed the world. His Spirit hovered over a lonely planet and affirmed its existence through words of creation. Even more intimately, He took man's dusty form and tenderly breathed into him the breath of life.

In creating the heavens and the earth, God showed that He isn't just some impersonal energy or all-pervasive force. He is a Person who exists for relationship, and He created you to begin a relationship with Him.

From the first chapters of your story, God has known you and has wanted you to know Him. If you don't know Him, perhaps you can become friends.

My soul thirsts for God, for the living God. When can I go and meet with God? —Psalm 42:2

Where True Intimacy Takes Place

A relationship exists when two or more parts come together to create a unified whole. Two people have one conversation. Several members make up one committee.

Marriage is, of course, the best example. A husband and wife can only be truly unified at their points of difference. What makes a partner "suitable" isn't that he or she is exactly the same. It's that their differences challenge and force each person out of his or her selfishness into the messy and life-giving proposition called intimate relationship.

Our relationship with God works similarly. It is in our *otherness* that true intimacy takes place. While man is created in God's image, he is not God. And God is far above what we could ever imagine.

But while in so many ways completely *other*, God still has entered into our frail existence and has invited us to join with Him in intimate relationship.

He invites you to know intimacy with Him and teaches you how to better find intimacy with those who matter.

The Word was God. . . . The Word became flesh and made his dwelling among us. —John 1:1, 14

The Promise of Relationship

What is the point of a promise?

Too often, we make a promise but never keep it. We promise to return that book and then see it years later in our yard sale box. We promise we'll pray for someone and forget to do so. We promise we'll stick with a friend through thick and thin but slowly go our own way.

God makes promises too. He promises He'll never leave us or forsake us. He promises that our lives will have purpose and meaning if we'll follow His way. He partners with us through *covenants* and makes His will known to us in *testaments*.

Is He trustworthy to keep His promises? The Bible certainly says so. Perhaps you have friends or family who say the same. It's risky to trust in such faithfulness if you've never seen it, but if your relationships are to have any promise, perhaps you can risk trusting in this God of the unseen.

There is a living God; he has spoken in the Bible. He means what he says and will do all he has promised. —Hudson Taylor

The Purpose of Relationship

Sometimes we wish everyone would just go away. The kids assume we're some bellhop there to serve their every need. Husbands or wives make constant demands on our time. Friends chat away on the phone, not understanding the pressures we're under.

But then we remember that we've been charged with caring for and protecting another human being. Who are we to be honored with such a responsibility? Sure, our spouse can be selfish, but so can we. Would we really be the person we are without him or her? And where would we be without friends who care enough to call and connect?

Here's a news bulletin: life can be difficult, and life has little meaning without each other. Without relationships, life will just be hard, and where's the joy in that?

Our relationships must start and end with God, the pure source of all faithfulness, intimacy, and promise. It's in relationship with Him where relationship finds its truest purpose.

The soul is not where it lives, but where it loves. —Thomas Fuller

Who You Were Meant to Be

You are nothing.

Sure, you're smart. You're an expert in your field. You're wise enough to see problems and avoid them. You have the vision to accomplish great things. You give a lot to charity, and you sacrifice for what you believe in.

But you also don't have much patience for people. You're not terribly kind. You're always tooting your own horn. You step on too many toes and have a short temper. You keep a list of people who've betrayed you.

No matter what you've accomplished, if you are not a person of relationship, if you are not a person of love, then who you are doesn't really matter.

Life is relationship. And love is the heart that gives relationship its life. God Himself is love. He doesn't just *love*; love is part of His very identity. When you love others with His love, then you *are* something. It becomes part of you too.

Become who you were meant to be.

> "By this all will know that you are My disciples, if you have love for one another." —John 13:35 *NKJV*

The Beginning of Love

Learning how to love usually begins with being loved by others.

Hopefully you were raised by loving parents and had family and friends who showed you love. If you weren't so lucky, consider that God has always loved you. Learn His story of love, and place yourself around people who know His love and want to pass it on.

God also wants you to love Him with everything you are. He understands that this will be a journey.

And God wants you to love others. But He's also patient. He understands the beginning of your love may be selfish. You know what you want and need. So just start by loving others the way you'd like to be loved.

Love had no beginning with God, but it *can* begin with you. It's never too late to start learning how to love.

"'Love the Lord your God with all your heart and with all your soul and with all your strength and with all your mind'; and, 'Love your neighbor as yourself.'" —Luke 10:27

One Small Kindness at a Time

Most often, love isn't rocket science. It can be as simple as greeting someone with a smile or asking the cashier how his day's been going or telling him that you appreciate the job he's doing. You may be shocked at the results.

Aren't you uplifted when someone reaches out to you with even the smallest kindness, especially when it's unexpected? Try doing the same for others.

You're not going to turn into Mother Teresa overnight. You'll love in the way only you can. But even Mother Teresa didn't love like Mother Teresa (based on our image of her superhuman feats of love). She loved others mostly with small kindnesses, and small kindnesses can collect into a lifetime of love.

Being a loving person is indeed a journey. Choosing to love others happens one small kindness at a time.

Do everything in love. —1 Corinthians 16:14

The Discipline of Love

Love is more than the sum of its parts. Is love an emotion? Of course. But love as an *action* is more than just expressing emotion.

When people show you love, you get all warm inside. That feeling will often motivate you to love in return. The problem is that if you wait for this feeling every time, you'll rarely love others as often as you need to.

The mark of maturity is to show kindness and care for others no matter how you're feeling. Parents soothing a crying baby at three in the morning certainly understand this. A wife betrayed by a cheating husband will find this notion much harder to swallow. But the principle remains the same.

The motivation to love must come from your discipline and commitment to the supreme value of personal relationship. In the end, knowing you've loved others well will make you feel far better than the finest poet could imagine.

When I do good, I feel good. When I do bad, I feel bad.
—Abraham Lincoln

Considering Others

The discipline of love usually shows up in our consideration for others.

At the checkout, most people drop their groceries, pay, and go. Few will look the cashier in the eye and realize that this is probably someone who's had a long day, receives a small paycheck, and may be weighed down by a load of burdens. No one stops to consider this person.

But the discipline doesn't stop at nothing. We're not just to pull ourselves out of our thoughts to consider the existence of another; we're also to consider them *more important* than we are.

So in this sense, *consider* doesn't necessarily mean *believe*. Too often, in our selfishness, we may not believe others are more important, but by an act of will and focus, you can consider them so. As an act of disciplined love, you can honor them with kindness.

It's a learned skill, to be sure. But the more you do it, the more you'll find that you're starting to believe they're more important too.

Do nothing out of selfish ambition or vain conceit. Rather, in humility value others above yourselves. —Philippians 2:3

Suffering with Others

What moves you to compassion?

When the world suffers a great disaster—an earthquake, a tsunami, a hurricane—people are often moved to compassion and they send money. Depending on how big the disaster is, they may send a lot of money.

But as much as we'd like to think otherwise, money doesn't really *cost* us anything. Is our compassion genuine? Probably. But the compassion that matters isn't so much a feeling for someone's suffering but rather joining them in it.

Hurricane Katrina was a good example. People sent a lot of money, and some dropped what they were doing and went to see what they could do. They showed up with medical aid, food, and water. They rebuilt homes. Most important, they sat and listened to those who'd lost everything. They provided comfort by their very presence.

This is the compassion that matters most—to join people wherever they are, especially when they're all alone in their suffering.

When Jesus saw her weeping . . . he was deeply moved in spirit and troubled. . . . Jesus wept. —John 11:33, 35

The Love That Matters

The standards of love are high—so high that it almost feels impossible to try.

Our patience runs too thin. Why should we be kind when no one's kind to us? It's hard to keep our cool when someone's asking for it. It's too difficult to forgive when we've been betrayed. Small kindnesses are possible at times, but how could we ever rise to the level of living a life of love, to give our very lives?

In order for your love to matter, you have to feed from the source of all love. God so loved that He gave His Son. His Son so loved that He gave His life. For you to have any chance at loving well, you simply need to give your life to God. Do that, and you'll be empowered to love as He has loved.

The love that matters will cost you. But you'll find no greater return on that investment.

"Love each other as I have loved you. Greater love has no one than this: to lay down one's life for one's friends." —John 15:12–13

In Search Of

WANTED: *Someone who understands me. Someone who will go with me to my favorite store even when they'd rather be somewhere else. Someone who won't talk when I want to be alone but will let me cuddle at a moment's notice. Someone who'll forgive me when I'm wrong and give me a break when I'm grumpy. I just need someone. Anyone. Please!*

Such an ad would scare away most people, but it's probably more representative of true romance than poetic words and flowers could ever be.

What's the romance most people are searching for? It's sharing life together. It's loving someone for who he or she is and being loved the same way. More than finding someone physically attractive, you want to find him or her attractive because he or she is pursuing a life that matters. Really, you're in search of a romance in which someone matters to you and you matter to him or her.

Try not to scare people away in your search, but don't lower your standards in choosing the one who will matter most.

I am my beloved's and my beloved is mine. —Song of Songs 6:3

First Dates

*Y*ou're surely overdressed. Or maybe underdressed? What will she be like? What will you be like? This is so nerve-wracking. There's the knock. You open the door.

This is a nice restaurant. Are you smiling too much? Okay, now you're talking too much. This feels like a job interview. Is your eye twitching? He is good-looking. That mole could be a deal-breaker.

You've said goodnight. *Was there a spark? It felt pretty good. Will he call? Maybe you should call. Is this second date material?*

First dates are a necessary evil. Why is it so hard? Some first dates crash and burn; others lead to second and third dates. And then, who knows?

Enjoy the journey of companionship in dating. Pray that you'll recognize those who warrant further investigation. Rest in God's plan for your future spouse. If it's one of your deepest desires, it's His too.

And, yes. You're the one who should call first.

How beautiful you are and how pleasing. —Song of Songs 7:6

A Time to Be Savored

You've exchanged *I love you*s. You've met each other's families. A proposal is around the corner, and you can't wait for life to begin.

Some debate the merits of a long engagement. If you know this is the one, why should you wait? But consider that your engagement shouldn't simply be about counting down to your nuptials.

The ritual of courtship is as important as your marriage will be, so it should be savored. Couples look back on this time as both unique to their relationship and all too short.

Long engagements can also be important because this choice should be tested by time. You need some life experiences under your belt. How does your fiancé react to life's challenges? How do you react as a couple?

Don't rush through the time of courtship and engagement. Every chapter in your love story should be enjoyed and handled with care.

There is a time for everything, and a season for every activity under the heavens. —Ecclesiastes 3:1

Marriage

You can't believe this person is yours.

Every fairy tale cliché is running through your head. Your shining knight. Your precious princess. There couldn't be a more beautiful wedding gown. Who could be more handsome in that tux? The candles. The music. It's all too perfect.

Well, the flower girl did toss her bouquet and run crying into her mother's arms. Your father must have had a cold for all that loud sniffing. The preacher mispronounced your last name, and you both tripped over your vows too many times to count. At least you got the kiss right.

We want marriage ceremonies to be perfect. But life isn't ceremony, and no marriage is perfect. The best marriages are both beautiful and messy, full of good intentions and bad manners.

But it's your beauty, your mess, no one else's. Forsaking all others and fighting for a lifetime of oneness. That's what matters.

A man leaves his father and mother and is united to his wife, and they become one flesh. —Genesis 2:24

Fighting for Unity

The silence has lasted days.

Why did you say those horrible things? And what about what your spouse said to you? Not worth repeating. How could two people so much in love try to destroy each other like that?

You're still sure you were in the right. But you can't sleep. You can't concentrate. If you can't be together, how much does being right matter?

If you want to get a good look at your selfishness, get married. The closer you are to someone, the harder it is to hide it, from them or from yourself. That's why God is so necessary for a marriage's success. Only God can help you overcome your selfishness to truly love another person.

The point in any argument isn't who's right. It's that God is the only one who's right. God wants you both to submit to Him and walk in unity.

Stop fighting each other. Do the romantic thing and fight for your unity.

Love is as strong as death, its jealousy unyielding as the grave. It burns like blazing fire, like a mighty flame. —Song of Songs 8:6

Fanning the Flame

This is a nice restaurant.

We haven't dressed up like this in a while. And we're both smiling. Should we call the babysitter? No. The kids are okay. We're actually talking. And boy, is my sweetie looking good. Maybe we can stop for custard on the way home.

Romance looks different when you're married. Much of the time it can look like pulling weeds together in the garden or you changing diapers while your spouse warms up the formula. But it's easy to forget that poetry and flowers and dinner dates are part of romance too.

Whether it's regular date nights or just random acts of kindness, you must flee the monotony of daily life and remind yourselves why that first date turned into a second and why you still matter to each other.

Once you get a good look at your spouse again across the restaurant table, it will come back to you.

Enjoy life with your wife, whom you love. —Ecclesiastes 9:9

To Know and Be Known

What is romance? Shared experience. Attraction. Feeling valued. Affection. Forgiveness. All these things. But ultimately, it is about knowing and being known.

Who knows more about you than your spouse? Your secrets. Your fears. Every little weakness. Every strength. And you know the same about your spouse. If you read a King James Bible, the word *knowing* is used for sexual relations. To know someone is to become one physically. But your mutual knowing is also emotional. It's spiritual. It's the best example of how we're meant to know intimacy with God.

True romance never happens without sacrifice. For a marriage to matter, you must each sacrifice your own way in order to become one. Likewise, Jesus sacrificed Himself so you could become one with God—a knowing, a communion that lasts for eternity.

Two lives join as one and create more life. There's no greater romance than that.

Now I know in part; then I shall know fully, even as I am fully known. And now these three remain: faith, hope and love. But the greatest of these is love. —1 Corinthians 13:12–13

Your Best Bonding Agent

The word *family* is often shorthand for everything that matters.

Your boss doesn't respect your abilities. Your coworkers come to you only when they have a complaint. But at the end of the day, you breathe a sigh of relief. You get to go home to your family.

You have good friends, but even with them, you have to put on a hat you wouldn't wear in the comfort of your own home. When you're with family, you wear many hats, but they're your favorite hats.

Family is the people you're around when you feel like you're home. Most often, but not always, family is those you're connected to through blood or marriage.

Even with all its human dysfunction, family can be your best bonding agent in a world of paper-thin connections. Family can be your best protection, your best motivation. Family can surround you, and family can be your launching pad for rocketing into the stratosphere of a life that matters.

> *Like arrows in the hands of a warrior are children born in one's youth. Blessed is the man whose quiver is full of them.*
> —*Psalm 127:4—5*

The Function of Dysfunction

Go beneath the skin of most anything, and you're probably going to find a complete mess. Cut into the human body, and you'll gasp at the mesh of tissue, bone, and organs. Crack open an electric gadget, and you'll scratch your head at the glob of wires and circuits.

Inside the walls of your average house is a complicated mess of human dysfunction. Family members who, for all their selfishness and conflict, don't look like they could serve any purpose or function that matters.

But consider that where the casual observer sees a mess of blood and guts or a tangled glob of wires, a doctor or a technician sees purpose and order, not to mention what the object's designer will see.

The dysfunction of family does have a function. You simply need to look to the Designer to understand what that function is.

He spreads out the northern skies over empty space; he suspends the earth over nothing. —Job 26:7

Worth a Second Look

Have you ever seen a movie and hated it but then, upon a second viewing, changed your mind? Usually it's because unmet expectations in your first viewing left you disappointed. But in being prepared for those flaws the second time around, you noticed what was good about the film, and maybe you ended up liking it.

How we view our parents is a bit like this. We grow up with high expectations for who they should be. But being the frail humans they are, they rarely meet those expectations. As you grow older, try giving them a second look. As long as you're aware of their flaws going in, you'll learn to appreciate their strengths.

How you view your parents matters. Perhaps most important, as your first caregivers and objects of love, your parents are your first picture of God. Could the way you see your parents affect the way you see God?

Maybe your parents aren't the only ones worth a second look.

Honor your father and your mother, so that you may live long in the land the Lord your God is giving you. —Exodus 20:12

Holding Fast to What Is Good

How you love your current family will be shaped by your connection to the family of your childhood. It will often shape who you choose for a spouse and your view of love.

If a son was nurtured by a mother of virtue, he'll often pursue a wife of similar caliber. If a little girl saw her father constantly scream at her mother, she may unwittingly choose a man who will scream at her too. If you were disciplined by reasonable parents, you'll likely pass this discipline style on to your own children.

You must recognize this connection and alert yourself to any existing misinterpretations of love. You should also affirm what was good about your upbringing and then negotiate with your spouse—who is similarly influenced by his or her childhood—to decide upon the best standard of love for your family.

Some connections should be upheld. Some broken. What matters is that you hold on to what is good.

Test all things; hold fast what is good. —1 Thessalonians 5:21 *NKJV*

Crossroads of Connection

The close kinship of brothers and sisters. The blissful memories of visiting grandparents and taking your kids to see your own parents. Aunts. Uncles. Cousins. Big Sunday meals. Holiday traditions. Weekend get-togethers and summer reunions.

Whenever possible, try to keep your connection to extended family. Your parents still have things to teach you and still want to know you love them. You'll always share with your brothers and sisters a tender communion that no one else understands. Keep in touch with that favorite aunt or uncle who loves the very sight of you.

As much as this great, big world can get away from us, extended families often feel bigger. It's nice to be reminded that you're a small cog in a sprawling generational machine.

It means you come from somewhere. It means that, no matter how adrift you might feel from day to day, you're part of something worth celebrating.

Family life is too intimate to be preserved by the spirit of justice. It can be sustained by a spirit of love which goes beyond justice.
—Reinhold Niebuhr

More Than the Family You Know

What do you do when your family isn't a family? Where do you turn when normal dysfunction turns into a never-ending cycle of abuse and toxic behavior?

All people—and therefore all families—can be brought back from the brink, so you shouldn't give up all hope. Find relief in knowing that there is more to family than the family you know. You can be adopted into another family.

God often did this when someone's family didn't measure up or when a person's future depended on being raised by another family. Moses was adopted by Pharaoh's family. The prophet Samuel was adopted. Jesus is God's son, but Joseph adopted Him as his own.

Sometimes we need a new family to love us, raise us up, and guide us to become someone who matters. This could be friends at church, a support group, or any community where people are pursuing what matters and where you feel like you're home.

Home is where you find it. And so is family.

"Whoever does the will of my Father in heaven is my brother and sister and mother." —Matthew 12:50

An Eternal Family

God would love to adopt you into His family.

While primarily revealed as a male, God demonstrates the traits of the best father *and* mother. He is fair and just, like a good father. He is a protector. He disciplines. Like the best mother, He is tender and nurturing. He instructs and guides with mercy and compassion.

God has a Son and understands what it means to love a child with everything you are. He loves you exactly the same way.

A relationship with God and His people isn't just about doing the right thing. It isn't just about improving your quality of life or going to heaven. A relationship with God and God's people is about family. Family makes everything matter, and God invites you into the family that matters most.

If you become part of God's family, you'll finally find your home, and your sense of family will never end.

God's dwelling place is now among the people, and he will dwell with them. They will be his people, and God himself will be with them and be their God. —Revelation 21:3

Fruit for Eternity

Parenting matters because it is probably our best picture of eternity.

Most of us feel a sense of longing to know that our contributions to life will outlive us, that we were put here not just to meet our own needs, but also to nurture and protect the growth and welfare of other human beings. Having and raising children answers that impulse. That the purpose of life is to be fruitful and multiply, to create more life.

An eternity without God is deprived of life and love. And so parenting without God too often regresses into animal instinct. You care for your offspring until they can fend for themselves, and then they're on their own.

But there is so much more to parenting, just as there is so much more to God. You are meant to bear fruit that will thrive and flourish beyond your span of days.

And your children can be reflections of eternity.

"Look up at the sky and count the stars—if indeed you can count them." Then he said to him, "So shall your offspring be."
—Genesis 15:5

The Fruits of Barrenness

Too many couples today suffer from the tragedy of infertility, or barrenness. But barrenness is nothing new. In the ancient Bible stories, God would sometimes intercede. In their helplessness, people turned to God, and He provided.

Ironically, this sense of barrenness doesn't stop when children finally enter the picture. In fact, in some ways, children only increase the need to rely on God in the midst of our helplessness.

Parenting strips you of your selfishness. It teaches you the true meaning of sacrifice. It brings you to your knees when you realize you can't always protect your children from pain or from the consequences of bad choices.

Your fierceness of love should remind you that God feels the same way. He loves you with everything He is and feels the same pain when you don't receive His provision and protection.

If you've felt at the end of your rope as a parent, use that barrenness to utterly rely on Him.

Trust in the LORD with all your heart and lean not on your own understanding. —Proverbs 3:5

Reflections in a Mirror

A big joy in parenting is that your children often share your looks, your mannerisms, and your talents. You burst with pride that who you are has been passed on to to this remarkable, precious human being.

But this reflection can also fill you with terror. You're not passing on just your strengths to your children, but also your weaknesses.

What do you see when you look in the mirror? Hopefully you admire what you see. But you probably also struggle with some insecurity and shame. The next time you look in the mirror, remember this: you were created in the image of God. That means you can rise above your weakness, and so can your children.

The more you can rest in the confidence of who you're becoming, the better you'll encourage your children to do the same.

By the grace of God I am what I am, and his grace to me was not without effect. —1 Corinthians 15:10

All for One and One for All

A husband and wife can live under the same roof and not really be married. They show up in public together, but in their private world, they're no more than roommates. They live separate lives in close proximity.

This happens in families as well. Parents may spend some quality time with their children in the early years. But when they're older, the parents live their lives, and the children live theirs. This family is not a family.

Of course, you can change this at any time. You can eat together, pray together. You can play together. You can let your children know that they belong, that they aren't going through life alone. You can start early if you still have small children. If your children are older, you can get to know each other again.

If two can become one, so can a family. Enjoy each other again.

This explains why a man leaves his father and mother and is joined to his wife, and the two are united into one. —Genesis 2:24 *NLT*

Talk, Talk, Talk

On an individual, parent-to-child level, perhaps the best thing you can do is talk. And talk. And talk some more.

This should start when your kids are very young. Read to them all the time. Engage them in their play. Ask them what they're thinking, and allow them to express their emotions. Most children will love to express themselves if asked.

As they grow older, kids may start to lose interest, but that's why you need to talk every day. If you start early and make it a normal activity, you'll build intimacy and trust that will last into the teenage years and beyond.

And when you talk, make sure you listen. These are human beings who deserve respect as much as they deserve nurturing and discipline. The more you listen, the more they'll ask for your guidance and the more they'll respect you and your authority.

If you want your children to pay attention, then from their earliest years, give them yours.

"See that you do not despise one of these little ones. For I tell you that their angels in heaven always see the face of my Father in heaven." —Matthew 18:10

To Make It Better

You love your children. When they fall down and get an owie, you want to kiss it and make it better. But you can't always protect them from the hurts of life. And because you love them, sometimes you shouldn't.

If your six-year-old carelessly breaks a favorite toy, don't run right out and get a new one. If your teenagers don't put their laundry in the hamper, they'll wear dirty clothes to school. By giving them a measure of freedom, you'll encourage them to take ownership for their behavior.

You should love them, talk, and share life with them far more than you discipline them. You'll need to choose your battles. You should hear their concerns as long as they're respectful, but endless arguments are a waste of time.

By providing firm and gentle discipline, you'll love them through their pain. Sometimes that's the best way to make it better.

No discipline seems pleasant at the time, but painful. Later on, however, it produces a harvest of righteousness and peace for those who have been trained by it. —Hebrews 12:11

The Head of the Household

To know any lasting peace as a parent, you'll need the wisdom to know the difference between what you can and should control in your children's lives and what you can't and shouldn't control.

This wisdom will come only by acknowledging who the true head of this household is: God Himself.

You'll make mistakes as a parent, but God can redeem those mistakes. Your children will fail many times growing up, but God will be best at disciplining, correcting, and welcoming them back home. You'll cry on your knees for the areas of parenting you can't control, namely their safety and their destiny, but that's all up to God.

If it's clear to your children that this is a family that serves the Lord, they'll more readily submit to you because you're submitting to Him. You'll raise a family that lives for eternity and honors the life that matters.

Can a mother forget the baby at her breast and have no compassion on the child she has borne? Though she may forget, I will not forget you! —Isaiah 49:15

Headed in the Same Direction

What is a friend?

Someone with shared interests? Someone who makes you laugh? Someone you can call at 3 a.m.? Your answers may vary depending on your perception of what matters. Some people take acquaintances for friends. Some have fair-weather friends who bail at the first sight of rain. Some isolate themselves and have few to no friends.

Once you start journeying toward what matters, you're going to need true friends. You'll face opposition. You'll lose confidence. You'll trip and fall. You're going to need friends to help share the burden of the journey.

But the friends you need most must be walking a similar journey. If you're headed in different directions, they won't understand where you're going, and they'll likely try to stop you. You'll live in constant temptation to compromise what matters in order to receive their acceptance.

How do you find the right friends? Step out on the road toward what matters. They'll be headed in the same direction.

One who has unreliable friends soon comes to ruin, but there is a friend who sticks closer than a brother. —Proverbs 18:24

What You Want Versus What You Need

It's good to have a diversity of friends.

Quiet friends who will calm you down. High-energy friends who will lift you up. Friends who will affirm what you believe and friends who will challenge your assumptions. It's good to have friends with whom you have everything in common and friends from different cultures and traditions.

Amid this colorful palette, try to include friends who walk wisely. In fact, try to make your wisest friends your closest friends.

Life is often a trade-off between what you want and what you need. Most of us desperately want friends, so we'll too often place compatibility above character. We want compatibility, but we *need* character. We need to have friends with wisdom to live the life that matters.

And when you put what you need first in your priorities, you'll usually find compatible friends as well.

Better is open rebuke than hidden love. Wounds from a friend can be trusted, but an enemy multiplies kisses. —Proverbs 27:5—6

True Acceptance

Your best friends are people you actually look forward to seeing. When their faces pop into your head, you cheer up. When you step into their house, the stress melts off you like ice chips on a warm day. You wear no masks and they put on none for you. Like your closest family, when you're with them, you're home.

True friends accept you for who you are. Acceptance matters. It's the fabric of love and companionship. You'll need unconditional acceptance for any friendship to rise above superficial fakery and hollow acquaintance.

Remember, though, that although everyone is running after acceptance, not everyone desires the life that matters. When you're with friends who do value that, their acceptance will ring all the truer. They'll accept you for who you are without any sense of condemnation, and they'll help you accept who you can become.

That's the acceptance that matters.

"Neither do I condemn you," Jesus declared. "Go now and leave your life of sin." —John 8:11

True Encouragement

The friends who matter will be your personal visionaries. When others see what's on the surface, true friends see you inside and out. When others pass you by on their way to their own agenda, those friends notice you and affirm your existence. When others doubt you'll amount to anything, your friends will see what you can be and will be your coach, cheerleader, or teammate.

They'll challenge you and allow you to challenge them. Remember, you're on this journey together, so your friends understand what's at stake. They will spur you on, encourage you, and push you. What would feel like judgment from others, feels like love from them.

They not only see in you what others can't; they often see what you're unable to see. If you trust the friend who points out what you can't see, you might try believing him or her, even if you don't like what they see.

Your best friends will encourage you—but remember that true encouragement will stretch you as much as it comforts.

Wounds from a friend can be trusted, but an enemy multiplies kisses. —Proverbs 27:6

Friends Who Lift You Up

They're right next to your spouse on speed dial. If you need to vent, they'll let you. If they offer advice, you take it. They'll meet you for coffee at a moment's notice or open their door to you if you've had a miserable day.

The friends who matter are an oasis in the desert of *I've had too much*. When you're at your weakest, they're the ones you turn to. When you're riddled with the bullets of the world's insensitivity, they'll be your sounding board but not your yes men.

And when the problem you're having isn't with the world, but with *you*—when you've messed up or fallen along the way—the friends who matter will be there for you then too.

They'll lift you up with a silly joke to get you out of your head and lift you up when you've fallen in another pit.

By the way, only friends on higher ground can lift you up. Find more friends like that.

A friend loves at all times, and a brother is born for a time of adversity. —Proverbs 17:17

Friends Who Stick with You

You've hit rock bottom.

One bad day turned into two. A week of funk became a month. A month of misery has become a season with no end in sight.

You've alienated most of those around you. Your fair-weather friends fled long ago. Even your family is at a loss and gives you your space. Most everyone has left you alone to wallow.

Except those friends who stick with you.

It may be one special friend, perhaps two. They'll talk or they'll listen, depending on what you can handle. As you share your jumbled feelings, they'll stare with a serious tenderness that makes it clear that they are sticking around, even when most others would probably leave.

On the journey to what matters, you will eventually hit a wall. And when you do, you'll need someone who won't run ahead with the others. They'll join you on the side of the road, bind your wounds, and help you move again.

One who has unreliable friends soon comes to ruin, but there is a friend who sticks closer than a brother. —Proverbs 18:24

The Knowing Look of Friendship

At the end of the *Lord of the Rings* movies, the hobbits are back from a long adventure, sitting in their hometown pub. High spirits and laughter surround them, but they sit quietly, looking at each other with knowing, weary smiles.

They share something their hometown friends will never know. They've journeyed long. They've struggled against evil. Somehow, they've returned victorious. The look they give each other is the knowing look of friendship, the battle-tested bond of joy and pain.

Jesus had friends—those who shared His journey, accepted Him, heard His wisdom and encouragement. Not all of them stuck with Him when He most needed it, but some did. And He restored most as friends again.

As you journey toward what matters, Jesus will come alongside and ask to journey with you. He knows the burden of your journey and will share all you need to complete it. Perhaps at the end of your journey, you'll exchange the knowing look of friendship too.

"I have called you friends, for everything that I learned from my Father I have made known to you." —John 15:15

 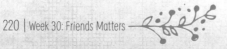

Outside Your Inner Circle

If quality relationships matter so much, shouldn't they infuse most areas of your life?

You can find quality relationship with your spouse, your family, your closest friends. But should these be the only areas of life that matter and the rest of your life is just an annoyance until you return to those who make you happy?

It's important for you to also live a life that matters with those outside your inner circle—to encounter and contribute to community groups that, like your closest relationships, are in some way following the same path that you are.

There's significance in calling yourself part of a larger community. It helps define your individual purpose, it gives you confidence knowing you're part of something larger, and it shows you how many disparate parts can create a unified whole.

Even your inner circle isn't big enough to contain the full scope of quality relationship. Start exploring communities that matter.

Do not forget to show hospitality to strangers, for by so doing some people have shown hospitality to angels without knowing it
—Hebrews 13:2

Sharing the Better Part of You

How often do you invite others to share in the delights of your home?

If you're like most, your home is one of your favorite places in the world. Wouldn't you want to share your favorite place with others? It gives them a chance to see you in your natural habitat, to learn more about what you love.

Hospitality is one of the best ways you can honor and celebrate other people. You tell them to kick off their shoes and offer them a nice beverage. You wait on them like they're a VIP at some posh restaurant. You show off your favorite décor or give them a tour of a scrapbook or photo album. You share personal stories of life in your family home.

But don't share your home only with family and friends. Honor your neighbors and new acquaintances with this gift as well. By inviting them into your house, you're honoring them with the better part of you.

The ornaments of your house will be the guests who frequent it.
—author unknown

Worship in Community

Some people look down on going to church. They'll say they can worship God during a nice round of golf on Sunday morning. While God can certainly be worshipped in nature, that's not the complete picture of what worship is meant to be.

Remember, God created us for relationship with Him, and worship is an important way to do this. But relationship with God is most often interconnected with how we relate to others. In this light, we're meant to worship in community with others.

Not every church will fit you. Find a church that takes the Bible seriously and where the worship speaks to you. But also look for a church where community and a sense of family are paramount. Church should be about living life together and joining others in pursuing what matters.

You may even find some new golfing buddies there. Just schedule your tee times for Saturday morning.

[N]ot giving up meeting together, as some are in the habit of doing, but encouraging one another. —Hebrews 10:25

Find Your Middle Ground

To get the complete benefits of quality relationship, you need to engage in community at all levels. It's good to feel like part of a large community, and most enjoy the company of a few close friends. But there's a middle ground you shouldn't neglect—the small group.

Whether it's a support group, a book club, or a Bible study, you'll discover the power of community in small groups in ways that you won't find elsewhere.

Groups of six to twelve people who meet regularly for food, friendship, and mutual enrichment will feel more like an extended family. Most introverts will be able to come out of their shells, and most extroverts will have enough social energy to satisfy. Overall, you'll have an additional support system beyond your inner circle that will encourage and sustain you.

Make sure it's a group pursuing what matters. And pray there's good coffee.

Every day they continued to meet together in the temple courts. They broke bread in their homes and ate together with glad and sincere hearts. —Acts 2:46

Service Groups

The more you start branching out beyond your inner circle of relationship by opening your home, joining a church, and spending time with a small group, you'll discover a pattern: one of the chief components of engaging in community is *service*.

You serve those invited into your home. Once you join a church, you'll be asked to serve. Support groups serve by their very nature. The phrase *community service* was not created out of thin air.

So make sure you find ways to serve in the communities you frequent. Better still, join communities whose sole purpose is service. Volunteer at a local mission. Join a group of mentors for disadvantaged children or adults. Join groups such as Habitat for Humanity to build houses for those in need.

It's one thing to serve alone. It's quite another to serve shoulder-to-shoulder with others. Relationship rises to a whole new level when you start working together for what matters.

In everything I did, I showed you that by this kind of hard work we must help the weak, remembering the words the Lord Jesus himself said: "It is more blessed to give than to receive." —Acts 20:35

The Engines of Community

If you're building your life on what matters, the engines of your community could also benefit from your involvement.

School boards, housing associations, charitable committees, and government offices—the expansive branches of community in your local town or county—are full of people who are thinking about the bigger picture.

Most of them understand that our society doesn't just function unaided. It takes people with a concern for local greenways, new traffic lights, commercial improvements, and sensible laws to keep the engines running smoothly.

You don't necessarily have to be highly educated or skilled to do your part. You simply need to care enough about your community to expand your horizons beyond work, friends, and family.

Local committees and government concerns may have existed beyond your scope in the past. But they do affect your life and the lives of those around you, so they matter. And they need more people who care about what matters to join their ranks.

Remind the people to be subject to rulers and authorities, to be obedient, to be ready to do whatever is good. —Titus 3:1

Communion

Relationship is about coming together. And coming together can be difficult. It feels hard enough to learn how to make our marriages work, to learn how to talk to our kids, to hold on to our closest friends. Who has the time to go beyond any of that and pay attention to the communities outside our circle?

But realize this: you need your community. Relating to those outside your circle can actually help your marriage, your kids, and your friendships. It can help to make your most important relationships work.

And also realize that your community needs you. Quality relationship isn't seen just through community but through communion, through diverse parts of God's creation working together. Our human communities must strive to do the same. There can be no communion if you don't play your role in the greater scheme of things.

Expand your vision for how you can join the human race in pursuing what matters.

The multitude of those who believed were of one heart and one soul . . . they had all things in common. —Acts 4:32 NKJV

Those You Don't Know

Perhaps you've made strides with your relationships. Your family is a priority. You nurture your friendships. You engage your community. But there's just one problem. Not many of your relationships include those with whom you have nothing in common.

There's another hill to climb regarding the relationships that matter—how well you seek out, welcome, and relate to strangers, those with different cultures, belief systems, and lifestyles than your own. Consider also those who are alone in their need—the social outcast, the economically disadvantaged, the chronically ill.

By honoring the different viewpoints or circumstances of another person, you'll discover you have more in common than you realize. The need for humility in what you believe. To let love rise to the forefront so you can find unity amid your differences.

Relationship is the currency that matters. Spend some of those dollars on people you don't know.

The stranger who dwells among you shall be to you as one born among you, and you shall love him as yourself; for you were strangers in the land of Egypt. —Leviticus 19:34 NKJV

To Never Know a Stranger

A well-mannered dog knows how to meet new people. He will approach strangers with a friendly excitement, tail wagging, tongue out, panting. *Look! It's someone new. Let's go greet them!*

Perfect strangers will stop with a brightened spirit and give him a soft scratch under the chin. They'll tell you what a sweet dog you have, and you'll share in warm fellowship and conversation.

Some people have this talent too. They've never known a stranger. The sight of a new person isn't something to ignore or fear. They make others feel valued with the warmth of their friendship.

While this comes more naturally to some, it can be learned by all. Start each day with a mission to reach out to those you don't know with warmth and personal interest. Have no agenda but simply to make this stranger your friend.

Whether you wag your tail or stick out your tongue is totally up to you.

"By this everyone will know that you are my disciples, if you love one another." —*John 13:35*

Safe Stretching

Stretching is a vital part of effective exercise. Not stretching leads to pulled muscles and torn ligaments. Some stretch too far and suffer injury as well. If you're going to exercise, you need to stretch all your muscles safely.

While all relationships will stretch you, relating to those with different ideas or backgrounds may stretch you the most. Don't imagine for a second that they have nothing to teach you. The first lesson is swallowing your pride so you can reach out to those different from you.

But just as your muscles are designed to tolerate only a certain range of motion, the same applies to your ideas and lifestyle. Reach out to strangers with love and acceptance, but also set boundaries for how far you're willing to go.

Stretching will give you more strength, flexibility, and energy in your relationships. Safe stretching will safeguard your health and wholeness to exercise what matters.

"I am sending you out like sheep among wolves. Therefore be as shrewd as snakes and as innocent as doves." —Matthew 10:16

Join Before You Invite

Too many people live their lives on the fringes. Their way of living or believing has left them marginalized, rejected by the mainstream of starched-shirt do-gooders. They may share the company of other outcasts, but they're otherwise entirely alone.

Jesus spent far more time seeking to include those on the fringes than those in the mainstream. He never compromised who He was, but He understood that living rightly starts with loving others deeply and without condition.

In reaching out to the outcast, you'll come to understand what that really means. You will remember that neither of you is deserving of God's love. God loves the outcast as much as He loves you.

But remember to join before you invite. Jesus joined people on the fringes before He ever offered God's acceptance. Join them where they are and in your mutual need for God. Then your invitation will ring all the more true.

"Be merciful, just as your Father is merciful." —Luke 6:36

Estranged to Their Need

There's another kind of outcast we tend to ignore. The homeless man who spends his nights in a shelter or sleeping under the bridge. The single mother with five kids, barely making it on food stamps and Medicaid. Maybe you are aware of them but don't know how to help. You can barely meet your own needs, not to mention the needs of someone you've never met.

But the lesson you learn in pursuing the relationships that matter is that your own needs are met more often when you meet the needs of others. Your awareness and compassion for such people is often all you need in order to help. These folks need your money and your ability to assist. But mostly they need you.

Show up. Make a new friend. And see where it goes from there.

> *"I was hungry and you gave me something to eat, I was thirsty and you gave me something to drink, I was a stranger and you invited me in, I needed clothes and you clothed me."*
> *—Matthew 25:35–36*

Breaking In to Their Prisons

Still another stranger is the one behind the walls of a prison.

Chances are, these men and women have hurt many people—and are usually also victims of abuse and addiction. They're trapped in an endless cycle of bondage. And most people have given up on them.

But there are other prisoners: the elderly, in nursing homes or suffering at home alone, wishing anyone would call; children stuck in foster care, longing for love and stability; or those trapped in depression or chronic illness, assuming their trial is theirs alone to bear.

For you to help, you'll have to enter the walls of their prison. Again, this may fill you with fear and inadequacy, but just as with the homeless or poor, simply showing genuine concern is 90 percent of what they need from you.

Prisons are not always man-made walls; sometimes they are the walls of the heart. You may be the one who releases a heart from the bondage of suffering alone.

"I was sick and you looked after me, I was in prison and you came to visit me." —Matthew 25:36

Breaking Down the Dividing Wall

Most women and some men enjoy a good chick flick. We enjoy the thrill of discovery in films like *When Harry Met Sally*. We want to hear how boy meets girl. The goal is getting them together so they'll live "happily ever after." But what happens after that? Most stories don't tell us.

God's story is more about what happens ever after. In the first two chapters, God meets Adam and Eve and they look like a great match. But then humankind leaves God, and the rest is about how they get back together.

Reaching out to strangers is a mirror of our story with God. All of us were once strangers to God. We held different beliefs, lived different lifestyles. We sat alone in our poverty, behind our prison walls. And God came to visit us in our aloneness.

He sacrificed everything so we would no longer be strangers. So we could live happily ever after.

[He] has destroyed . . . the dividing wall of hostility. . . . He came and preached peace to you who were far away and peace to those who were near. —Ephesians 2:14, 17

Words of Relationship

If you're going to uphold a life where relationship matters, you do need to build on your relationship with God. But how do you get to know someone you've never seen?

Reading the Bible is a start. It is His book. The words are the fruit of His relationship with man. God related intimately with human beings and inspired words to be read by future generations like ours.

Is the Bible a book of rules? Yes, it has rules. Is it a book of stories? Yes, many, many stories. But it's more a book about relationship—how God desires relationship with us and the results of accepting or rejecting that relationship. More important, it's a book that leads to relationship.

How do you relate to this unseen God? You start by relating to His words of relationship. They have been seen and can be known.

Sovereign LORD, you are God! Your covenant is trustworthy, and you have promised these good things to your servant.
—2 Samuel 7:28

Speed Dating

In speed dating, singles spend only a few minutes in conversation with potential partners before moving on to the next. The intention is to rely on intuition and first impressions to determine whether you should give a relationship a chance.

It's an interesting idea, but it inflates the fantasy of love at first sight, and it potentially belittles another person through superficial judgment. Intimacy isn't just about that initial spark of attraction. It is a carefully sewn fabric crafted through years of conversation and shared experience.

Perhaps you've practiced some speed dating with God. Give Him a chance. Read His book—not just a verse here and there; return to it daily.

Talk to Him. You can say anything you like. Ask Him questions, and listen for an answer. Don't make your chats few and far between. Years of conversation and shared experiences will be required.

God deserves more than just your first impressions. Give Him a chance.

Beware lest we mistake our prejudices for our convictions.
—*Harry Ironside*

So Easy to Love

Who are the people you love?

Usually, your parents are your first loves. They gave you life. You've always known them. While hardly perfect, they provided for your every need. They made you who you are today. As an adult, you've learned to love others as well. You love your spouse like no other. You love your kids beyond imagining. You love your friends.

Perhaps as you were growing up, you heard that God gave you life. You've always known about Him. You've wondered how perfect He could be, and you've heard He will provide for your every need and make you who you're meant to be.

Just like you did with your spouse and children and friends, perhaps now you can learn to love Him too. Get to know God and see if He's worth loving.

What makes it so easy to love your family and friends is that they love you. And so does God. Perhaps that's the first thing you need to know about Him before you consider loving Him in return.

We love because he first loved us. —1 John 4:19

The Main Object of Your Desire

We want to please those we love most. Wives join their husbands on golfing trips. Husbands sit patiently on mall benches outside boutiques. Parents attend soccer matches in the wind and rain. We do things like this when the object of our love is more important than our sacrifice or discomfort.

As you grow to know God better, you grow to love Him more too. You'll find that the promises you read about in His Word start coming true. You'll be less cynical about Him and more grateful for how much He cares for you. Your focus in following Him will become less about obligation and more about adoration.

It's true that God knows far better than we do how we should conduct our lives. It becomes a lot easier to trade your desires for His when He becomes the main object of your desire.

"If you love me, keep my commands." —John 14:15

For Better or Worse

Perhaps you're under the impression that for you to show proper love and respect for this supreme Creator, you always have to *make nice*. Maybe you think you can't ever show that you're angry with God, confused, or frustrated. But not showing these emotions would be lying because we all feel this way sometimes.

The Bible is full of such examples. People complain to God. They bargain. They argue with Him. They cry out in anger and frustration with their plight. Jacob actually wrestled with God, demanding His blessing.

Genuine intimacy is always the product of healthy conflict resolution. If you can't be open about your differences, your relationship will be no more than a polite fabrication.

Don't be afraid to confront God when you're angry, worried, or confused. He can take it. Just as with your other important relationships, if you're going to love God for a lifetime, you must love Him for better or worse.

"Your name will no longer be Jacob, but Israel, because you have struggled with God and with humans and have overcome."
—Genesis 32:28

Making Up with God

It's hard to stay mad at the one you love forever.

You truly let God have it. You and He have not been on good terms. But after a while, you realize that maybe you were too quick to judge. Maybe you could be more patient with His timing and make more of an effort to understand His ways.

You also remember that you're no picnic at times either. You've ignored Him more than you'd like to admit. You've had your own agenda in this relationship. When you've owned up to this in the past with Him, He's forgiven you.

Perhaps He means more to you than you've wanted to admit. Perhaps He's done more for you than, in your anger, you chose to accept. After all, you love Him and He loves you.

You've had no more important relationship than the one you've had with Him. Maybe it's time you two made up.

For his anger lasts only a moment, but his favor lasts a lifetime;
weeping may stay for the night, but rejoicing comes in the morning.
—Psalm 30:5

Choose Relationship

What distinguishes heaven from hell?

Heaven is about eternal relationship—God in blissful, intimate harmony with humankind and humankind with each other. And hell? Some say fire and outer darkness. But the chief torment will also be defined by relationship. Utter aloneness. Forever separated from any relationships that matter.

God calls to us our whole lives, inviting us to taste heaven in the here and now—to know harmony with Him and harmony with each other. But some of us will choose hell in the here and now. We will choose to be alone. Although surrounded by others, we have no relationships that matter. If we remain alone until our final breath, God mournfully honors that choice as we pass into eternity.

You don't have to be alone. You aren't meant to be alone. No matter the hell you've known, choose relationship and your heaven can begin right now.

The only air of the soul, in which it can breathe and live, is the present God and the spirits of the just: that is our heaven, our home, our all-right place. —George MacDonald

PART 5:

WHAT'S WRONG AND HOW TO MAKE IT RIGHT

To Yearn for What Is Right

What's wrong?

What's wrong with the world? What's wrong with people? What's wrong with you?

Most people ask these questions on too regular a basis. We look at the world and want to pull our hair out for all the senselessness. We can't imagine the things that people do for the most meaningless reasons—and, to our frustration, why *we* do what we do may be the greatest mystery of all.

What's wrong isn't right, but it can be made right. The world will be made right, but if you're like most, that's beyond your scope and control. What about other people? For the most part, you can't make them right either. But you can look to yourself.

What's wrong matters. It alerts you to the absence of what is right, and if you're listening, that absence should alert you to your yearning for what is right.

Truly yearning for what is right is where this journey begins.

Creation has been groaning as in the pains of childbirth. . . . We wait eagerly for our adoption to sonship, the redemption of our bodies. —Romans 8:22–23

What We See as Trouble

There's actually more to the *Serenity Prayer* than is usually recited in recovery meetings. One powerful line says that serenity comes from "accepting hardship as a pathway to peace."

Another way you could put that is: *what we see as trouble, God sees as opportunity*.

If you believe in God, perhaps you also believe that He created everything you see. Then perhaps you'll consider that God is in the business of seeing all He has created, both the good and the bad, as opportunities to accomplish His purposes in history.

And that includes your troubles.

So rather than simply mourning what's wrong with the world, you can allow God to turn your troubles into opportunities to make things right.

If you do, your troubles will no longer be something to hide from. They'll become opportunities to see as God sees.

God works for the good of those who love him, who have been called according to his purpose. —Romans 8:28

The Paralysis of the Soul

Famous for the role of *Superman*, Christopher Reeve was a towering picture of strength. Sadly, he suffered a critical injury in 1995, paralyzing him from the neck down. The man of steel then became famous for advocating for research to find a cure for paralysis.

One of the chief dangers of paralysis is that you're unable to feel any pain. If you suffered a cut in your leg and were all alone, you'd be unaware of the wound. Unable to feel pain, you could die from bleeding or infection without ever knowing why.

When you suffer significant injuries to your soul, this can leave you paralyzed to feeling emotional pain. But no matter how deep it is, pain still has a purpose. It alerts you to the need for attention and healing. It reminds you that something needs to be made right.

You may not feel your wounds, but they can still kill you. Fortunately, unlike Reeve's condition, the paralysis of the soul has a cure.

I consider that our present sufferings are not worth comparing with the glory that will be revealed in us. —Romans 8:18

The Opportunity in Loss

They just foreclosed on your house. Where will you live? Your 401(k) just took a nosedive. How will you retire? Your spouse just told you she's leaving you. How can you possibly go on?

All of us will experience loss. Sometimes the loss is legitimate, as will be the pain that follows. Sometimes the loss is a wake-up call that what you were clinging to so tightly doesn't matter. But no matter what we lose, with the pain of loss comes an opportunity.

The opportunity in loss is that your choices become simpler, your focus more singular. When everything is stripped from you, you can choose to despair, or you can choose to finally surrender to the only One who can make things right.

What you're really surrendering is your definition of what matters. You live on more than God, but God is all you need. Suffering loss is often the best gateway to that epiphany.

"What good is it for someone to gain the whole world, and yet lose or forfeit their very self?" —Luke 9:25

A Righteous Anger

What makes you angry? Squeaky shopping cart wheels? People who talk during movies? Unwrapping a new music CD? Some people stay angry over these kinds of annoyances.

How about when your baby won't stop crying? Or when your spouse is late for dinner? Or when your coworker keeps making the same mistake? That's the kind of anger most people would admit they need to keep in check.

What about con men who rob innocent investors of their nest eggs? Or husbands who beat wives? Or the latest news about child sex trafficking? Hopefully, that makes you angry. And that's an anger that can be used.

A righteous anger is an anger that longs for what is wrong to be made right. It should ignite in you a fire to see the helpless protected, the brokenhearted healed, and the captives freed.

Too often, evil thrives because people aren't angry enough. Channel your righteous anger into doing something about it.

The Lord became angry with Solomon because his heart had turned away from the Lord, the God of Israel. —1 Kings 11:9

The Still, Small Voice

There is an invisible blanket around you. Thick, heavy. Your mind feels empty and filled with cotton at the same time. Your eyes ache. Sleep, when you can find it, is your only relief from this dull, ever-present ache.

You're suffering deep depression. You don't even care anymore. People will suggest medications or yoga or getting a dog, but you feel as though there's nothing that can be done.

And in that nothingness, God is there. God is the only living Being ever to dwell amid nothing and win. God can speak loudly and with fanfare. But usually He speaks in a still, small voice, and you have to become very still and very quiet in order to hear it. When you are deeply depressed, that's an opportune time to hear Him.

Just stay where you are, and allow yourself to be covered by God's wings of solace and protection until what's wrong can be made right again.

I will take refuge in the shadow of your wings until the disaster has passed. —Psalm 57:1

The Ultimate Wrong Made Right

What about the pain of death? It is a wretched assault on everything that matters, particularly when the life of a young or innocent person is taken from us. But although grief is our greatest pain, it really isn't different from any other pain. In our grief, there are still opportunities to be seen.

How precious would life be to us if there were no cost, if there were no limitations or end to it? When we experience death, life becomes a frail and wondrous thing to be enjoyed above all else.

God also saw death as an opportunity. He sent His young and innocent Son to die on the cross so that death would be no more.

Even something as wrong as death matters when we see it as an opportunity to remember that all things will one day be made right. In the midst of your grief, you can still see as God sees.

For now we see only a reflection as in a mirror; then we shall see face to face. Now I know in part; then I shall know fully, even as I am fully known. —1 Corinthians 13:12

Weakness

We're not supposed to be weak, some say. Weakness is frowned upon. You have to be strong to make the team. You have to be strong to climb the corporate ladder and overcome obstacles.

So we try to be strong. We put on the face of strength when we go to work. We wear the "I've-got-it-all-together" suit at church. We smile and say, "Fine," when friends ask how we're doing. But we're not always strong. In ways we'll never admit to others, we're weak.

By admitting your weakness, you'll discover another opportunity—a chance to stop trying to be strong in your own strength and to seek your strength from God. What's wrong with the world and ourselves is often rooted in people trying to strive in their own strength. The only way to find the strength to truly make things right is to trade your weakness for His strength.

You have to admit, that's a pretty good deal.

He said to me, "My grace is sufficient for you, for my power is made perfect in weakness." —2 Corinthians 12:9

A New Egg

Most people have heard the nursery rhyme as a child: "Humpty Dumpty sat on a wall. Humpty Dumpty had a great fall. All the king's horses and all the king's men couldn't put Humpty together again." For too many of us, this has become less childhood fantasy and more like a prophecy.

We feel fatally flawed. We're born fragile eggs. We're fated to sit on narrow walls and to have great falls. We're destined to remain forever broken.

This is the other extreme in how we see our weaknesses. Some people ignore their weaknesses; others use them as an excuse to give up on ever trying to put the broken pieces back together.

But there's a difference between Humpty Dumpty's king and the King of heaven. The King of heaven created you. And no matter how fragile you are or how great your fall, He can *re-create* you.

Slowly but surely, He'll put you together again.

"Very truly I tell you, no one can see the kingdom of God unless they are born again." —John 3:3

Acceptance Versus Expectation

Many of us are more than aware of certain flaws—age spots, the newest wrinkle, the distorted shape of our nose. And we are also aware of the internal flaws—a lack of discipline, selfishness, how often we've tried and failed.

We shouldn't ignore our weaknesses, but it matters how we interpret them. Our best interpretation comes from knowing the difference between *acceptance* and *expectation*.

You've seen the tension in those you love and respect. Your parents. Your favorite teacher or coach. They accept you for who you are, flaws and all. But they also expect more of you. They want you to rise above, accomplish, and overcome.

God is the same way. He made you and accepts you for who you are. But He also expects you to reach higher to experience the life that matters.

Rest in the peace of God's acceptance. And use His expectations for your life to trade your imperfect ways for His perfect will and care.

"I do not give to you as the world gives. Do not let your hearts be troubled and do not be afraid." —John 14:27

Condemnation Versus Conviction

There's another area of interpretation necessary when considering your weaknesses: *condemnation* versus *conviction*.

How do you feel when you look at your weaknesses, flaws, or mistakes?

Do they make you feel like giving up? Like you're worthless or incapable of change? That's condemnation. You've passed final judgment and essentially condemned yourself to death.

Or are the feelings more like fuel to a fire than a hammer to the head? Do you regret your mistakes enough not to repeat them? Do your failures make you not want to give up but rather try all the harder? Then what you're feeling is probably conviction.

Both condemnation and conviction will feel similarly painful. But it's what they lead you to do that will determine whether looking at your weaknesses is a waste of time or a powerful method for pursuing the life that matters.

Godly sorrow brings repentance that leads to salvation and leaves no regret, but worldly sorrow brings death. —2 Corinthians 7:10

Beyond the Shadows of Doubt

Some people believe, as with weakness, they're not supposed to reveal their doubts, so they cover them up with a false confidence. The problem is that the beliefs they pretend to display aren't truly beliefs but an act to gain the approval of others.

Others are frozen by doubt. They think that if they have any doubt about something, it's doomed to fail. So they never really believe in anything or do anything worth believing in.

The most important kind of faith is the trust you have for another person. If that trust is in God, you can learn to have faith in His faithfulness. So while your world may still be full of doubt, the object of your trust isn't.

In this way, your doubts don't have to be a reason *not* to believe. They can be a reason to believe all the more.

[Abraham] faced the fact that his body was as good as dead. . . .
Yet he did not waver through unbelief regarding the promise of
God, but was strengthened in his faith and gave glory to God.
—Romans 4:19–20

The Mirror You Should Be Looking Into

It makes sense that in order to move from weakness to strength, we should first look at ourselves. We should take a good, hard look in the mirror and see what we see.

Looking at ourselves can be helpful in reflecting on our behavior and in understanding how we see ourselves. But too often, we become preoccupied with the image we see. We worship our strengths and think we don't need change, or we despair over our weaknesses, thinking we'll never change.

That's why there's another mirror we should look into. We should reflect on God's image. This is done through worship, prayer, meditating on Scripture, and seeing God in His creation.

God's image projects nothing but light. When you look into an image that reflects light, that light reflects back on you. By no effort of your own, you begin to glow with the strength of God.

What mirror are you looking into? Find your strength by looking into His.

We all, who with unveiled faces contemplate the Lord's glory, are being transformed into his image with ever-increasing glory.
—2 Corinthians 3:18

Running in God's Strength

You begin your run. You choose a pace as your feet contact the concrete. You move your arms. Your breathing quickens. Your calves start to burn. Your muscles ache. Your breath becomes an engine. You focus on the rhythm of your feet. No matter how weak you feel, you're going to make it to the end.

There's another type of weakness that matters—the weakness you feel when you step out to tackle what is difficult, seeking to build your stamina and strength to run the race for what matters. You press on because reaching the goal is more important than your weakness.

Running in God's strength won't be easy. You'll feel the pain of change, of being challenged by your weaknesses to move beyond your passive life of ignoring what's wrong and running toward what's right.

Run the difficult race. The weakness you feel will become an opportunity to focus on your next steps and to strive ever harder for the finish line.

Endurance is not just the ability to bear a hard thing, but to turn it into glory. —William Barclay

Healing

Most of the time, you don't even notice it. But it's there: that dull throb of pain. The wound runs so deep in your bones and tissue that it's become part of who you are. You've medicated to forget about its presence. You've developed a tough exterior to protect yourself from similar wounds. But no matter what you do, the wound remains.

What could be the use in opening old wounds? It's true that it would be worthless if there were no chance that the wound could be healed.

But there is One who can heal even your deepest wounds. He was wounded too. Although He was healed of those wounds, He still bears their marks as a reminder.

Imagine life free of coping with that ever-present pain. Imagine this wounded Healer making all those wrongs right once more.

He was wounded for our transgressions, He was bruised for our iniquities; the chastisement for our peace was upon Him, and by His stripes we are healed. —Isaiah 53:5 *NKJV*

Do You Want to Be Made Well?

Sometimes the wounds you carry seem like old friends. When you decide something's here to stay, you grow accustomed to it. After a while, they become a type of security blanket. In a bit of twisted irony, you can't imagine life without them.

It may seem like an insulting question, but it needs to be asked: Do really want to be healed of your past hurts? Do you want to be made well?

If you didn't immediately answer, then you're probably believing a lie. Those past hurts aren't your friends. Leaving them behind won't be the death of you. You didn't deserve to receive that pain, and you aren't fated to live with it forever.

Come to terms with any resistance you may have to being healed because you'll have to take some action in order to receive it.

When Jesus saw him lying there, and knew that he already had been in that condition a long time, He said to him, "Do you want to be made well? . . . Rise, take up your bed and walk." —John 5:6, 8 NKJV

Mistaking Symptoms for the Cause

There's no cure for the common cold. So when people get sick, they mainly look to survive the symptoms. As long as they're not overcome with coughing, sneezing, and blowing their noses, they make an attempt to function.

Too often, with our emotional or spiritual wounds, we mistake the symptoms for the cause and try to address only the surface of things.

We're constantly irritated with our children, not realizing the impact of our father's anger toward us. We're less patient in our second marriage, not understanding that we carried the wounds of the previous marriage into the new. We suffer from chronic anxiety, yet our restlessness is caused by hurts from long ago.

No matter how well you've learned to manage your pain, it still affects you. Consider that some of your present "sickness" could be a symptom that deeper wounds are untreated. Spend more time addressing the cause rather than just treating the symptoms.

People look at the outward appearance, but the LORD looks at the heart. —1 Samuel 16:7

Understanding and Ownership

If you had been fated to suffer the wounds of your past, would that let you off the hook for who you are today? Should you continue to wallow in your pain? Or if those wounds were just about the environment you grew up in, can't you just choose a new environment to find healing?

Who you are today is probably the product of both destiny and environment. So the key to your healing will be through *understanding* and *ownership*.

You can't change your past, but you can seek to understand how your past wounds affect you in the here and now. With this understanding, you can then take ownership for who you are today. You can accept responsibility for your current behavior while seeking all the more to find healing for those past hurts.

Understand that you weren't designed for pain only, but also for healing. Take ownership for your healing with the strength of that conviction.

"Ask and it will be given to you; seek and you will find."
—*Matthew 7:7*

The I AM of Healing

Bbut the question remains: If you can't change the past, how can your past wounds be healed?

If a physician had the technology, he could heal any wound. But the difficulty with an emotional or spiritual wound from your past is that even if it is removed, the cause of the wound still remains. It seems you can never be free of it.

But consider this: God is a physician who works outside of time. His personal name in Scripture is *I AM*. He is ever-present and also eternal. So He doesn't see your life as past, present, and future. When He heals you, He can heal every part of you.

It's a mystery how we can live in time and yet also find such an eternal healing. But our job isn't to understand. Our job is to live in His eternal presence and allow Him to heal our past, present, and future.

Forgetting what is behind and straining toward what is ahead, I press on toward the goal to win the prize for which God has called me heavenward in Christ Jesus. —Philippians 3:13–14

The Best of Both Worlds

Who makes the best counselor? Not the people who ask you to rise to their level without ever having lived in the pits. You also don't want advice from those who have suffered but haven't made real strides to rise above where they are and find true healing.

Usually the best counselor is one who is standing in a place of healing and wholeness and has reached those heights from the lowest places. He or she has come from a place of pain and has found the path to overcome.

With God you get the best of both worlds. His Son has been where you are. He has suffered in every way you have. But He now lives in the heavenlies and invites you to share in the healing.

Identify with the one who can identify with you. He knows your pain and can show you exactly how to rise again from the ashes of your pain.

It is by Christ you have been saved. And God raised us up with
Christ and seated us with him in the heavenly realms.
—Ephesians 2:5–6

Naked and Unashamed

So far, this has been more an invitation to healing; the *how* of healing will follow.

Are you starting to have a vision for your healing? What will you look like when so many wrongs are made right? One place to look is to the beginning, before pain ever existed. The Bible says that man and woman walked the earth naked and unashamed. Can you imagine? To be completely open to God and others—whole and content with everything you are?

Part of what God did in sending His Son was to offer us a return to this state of innocence, where we too can walk naked, feeling no shame—perhaps physically but certainly emotionally and spiritually. This healing won't be complete until that original paradise is one day restored. But the process can begin, and the benefits can be enjoyed starting now.

Your road to healing may be a long one, but if you're willing and you believe, your life will never be the same.

Adam and his wife were both naked, and they felt no shame.
—*Genesis 2:25*

The How of Healing

The most fundamental *how* of emotional and spiritual healing is found in the act of forgiveness.

Life is relationship, and when your relationships are broken, life seems broken. Forgiveness restores or heals that which is separated. It restores how your mind, emotions, and spirit should relate to each other. It restores the way you're meant to relate to God and others.

Only when a husband and wife practice forgiveness can their relationship be healed of its wounds. Only when an adult child learns to forgive the sins of his or her parents, can he or she truly be restored to walk as a complete man or woman. Only when you learn the art of seeking forgiveness from God and understand how much He wants to forgive you can you truly be healed—body, mind, and soul.

The how of healing is forgiveness. At times it will feel like an invasive and risky procedure, but it's a matter of life and death.

Confess your sins to each other and pray for each other so that you may be healed. —James 5:16

Asking for Forgiveness

Often we look at our wounds and think only of what others have done to us. While healing our wounds requires forgiving others, the focus should begin with our own need for forgiveness.

This may not feel just, but it is practical. You'll never find healing while waiting for others to come to you. You can't control what people do; you can only control yourself. So you need to first address how you've contributed to your own brokenness and the role you've played in your broken relationships.

This starts with asking God for forgiveness. He's your most important relationship that needs healing, and when you find restoration with Him, you usually also restore yourself.

You'll be humbled by this process, but in it you'll find the motivation and the ability to ask for forgiveness from others, as well as start learning how to offer forgiveness.

"For if you forgive other people when they sin against you, your heavenly Father will also forgive you." —Matthew 6:14

Justice and Mercy

Once you've begun seeking forgiveness from God and others, it will be easier to start offering forgiveness. But there will still be the exceptions. Some wounds are too deep, some hurts too horrific. We want justice for what has been done to us.

But consider this: justice has been served, but through a story twist that Hollywood could never conceive, God's innocent Son was fatally wounded in payment for every hurt that has been inflicted upon you, for every hurt you've caused yourself.

God is able to look beyond what we all deserve because the ultimate justice was inflicted against the only person who deserved none. In one moment in time, justice was served, and forgiveness and mercy became available to all who would receive it.

Surrender your human sense of justice to that supernatural act of mercy, and you'll find an ability to forgive others that could only come from above.

All have sinned and fall short of the glory of God, and all are justified freely by his grace through the redemption that came by Christ Jesus. —Romans 3:23–24

Own Your Stuff and Offer Grace

Here's another way to describe forgiveness: *own your stuff and offer grace.*

The most wounded relationships usually include people who are always first to point the finger and last to take responsibility. Your husband *always* does this or that! Your mother *never* did that! We blame. We deflect. The pain remains and the distance grows wider.

If you're waiting for others to come to you, if you're waiting for justice to be served, you'll never be at peace with others or with yourself—someone needs to be the bigger person. Since you can't control what others do, that someone should be you.

But really, the biggest person is God. Ask God for the courage to humble yourself when it's the last thing you want to do. And usually, the more often you own your stuff and offer grace, the more you'll see it returned in kind.

> *"Do to others what you would have them do to you."*
> —*Matthew 7:12*

Loving Your Enemy

Forgiveness is one thing. Getting along is another.

There are people you just can't stand. You're pretty sure they talk about you behind your back. You don't respect them, and they don't respect you. You suppose you can forgive them for their selfish, vindictive ways, but their very existence still irritates you like an itch you can't scratch.

The life that matters is about going above and beyond, including with your enemy. Stop dehumanizing this person as simply an object of your annoyance. He or she is to be valued and loved just like anyone else.

No matter how strong the indifference or hate, it will cower in the face of love. Smile the next time you see that person—and mean it. Ask how she's doing. Bring him a gift and expect nothing in return. Take her to lunch and ask her to tell you her story.

You may just shock this person into an unlikely friendship.

"Love your enemies and pray for those who persecute you, that you may be children of your Father in heaven." —Matthew 5:44–45

When the Distance Is Too Great

How do you forgive or seek forgiveness when the distance is too great?

Sometimes the distance is necessary: an estranged spouse or someone who seriously hurt or abused you. The distance may be permanent, such as a parent who has died. Or maybe the distance can't be helped: those who'd never admit their wrongs or receive your admission of wrongdoing.

What do you do in these situations?

While the ideal scenario is for two parties to forgive each other, how they respond to you or even their presence shouldn't stop you from asking for forgiveness or offering yours. The very act from your side of things can bring healing. Some people write a letter and never send it. Some people sit down and speak to an empty chair.

However you do it, don't let a little distance keep you from the healing you desperately need.

You who once were far away have been brought near by the blood of Christ. For he himself is our peace, who has made the two groups one and has destroyed . . . the dividing wall of hostility.
—Ephesians 2:13—14

The Beauty Is in the Making

Quilts are a celebration of love, family, hearth, and home. They cover marriage beds or are hung on walls to bring color to a room. The different patterns often tell a family history. They speak of the warmth of unity and the hope of legacy.

But perhaps the chief beauty behind quilts is in their making. These different—often *very* different—blocks are patched together to find a unified whole. Sometimes it doesn't seem like they could ever work together, but once the pattern is complete, there is only warmth and beauty to behold.

We are all patchwork quilts. If we allow Him to, the Master Craftsman can patch us together into a pattern that just works. Love, grace, and forgiveness are the threads that bind, making us whole, healing us once again.

Live a life of forgiveness. The beauty is in the making.

Where there is hatred let me sow love; where there is injury,
pardon; where there is doubt, faith; where there is despair, hope;
where there is darkness, light; where there is sadness, joy.
—*St. Francis of Assisi*

The Look of Healing

If forgiveness is the how of healing, openness is the look of healing.

When you're forgiven and know how to forgive others, there's nothing to hide anymore. You don't have to put on masks, build walls, or burn bridges. People in the process of being made whole are more open. They're more open about who they are to themselves, to God, and to others.

Forgiveness frees you from the bondage of brokenness, but openness is the key to maintaining it and ensuring that your healing proceeds on schedule.

The more transparent you are about your pain, the quicker your healing will occur. And the whole person, whose wrongs are being made right, is an open book. You are free to be who you are and free to become who you're meant to be.

Every Genesis has a Revelation. If you really want to be made well, your great revealing can begin right now.

Then Peter came to Jesus and asked, "Lord, how many times shall I forgive my brother or sister who sins against me? Up to seven times?" Jesus answered, "I tell you, not seven times, but seventy-seven times." —Matthew 18:21–22

The Real You

There's an unexpected consequence that comes from our pain. When we get hurt, we set up walls for protection. We detach our heads from our hearts so we won't feel anymore. We take on a false identities or outrageous behaviors to divert attention from who we really are.

But the problem is that you're not just hiding the real you from others; you are also hiding from yourself. Discover your walls and start tearing them down. Find out how to feel again. Root out your false identities and erratic behaviors. Don't do this for others but for your own self-discovery.

Who is the real you? You may not remember. There is probably both ugliness and a striking beauty. You are likely both frail and powerful. Confused and full of passion. An unformed child and a seasoned warrior.

Open up to yourself, and discover who you really are. It will be an exhilarating wonder to behold.

"You can't keep your true self hidden forever; before long you'll be exposed." —Luke 12:2 MSG

Opening Up to Others

It's one thing to open up to God and another to open up to yourself. But to others? Why is that necessary? If God is the one who heals you, why should you risk baring your soul to others only to have it trampled?

First, it's God who will ultimately heal you, but the primary way He works is *through* people. Most often, God will heal you through the words and care of people just like you.

Second, remember that healing is about relationship. Many married couples struggle, and then on their first visit to a marriage support group, they're shocked to discover how many couples share the same challenges they do. The best way to heal your relationships is to start relating to those who need similar healing.

For you to become a person of sound mind and body, you need to be open with others, and they need to be open with you.

> *We loved you so much, we were delighted to share with you not only the gospel of God but our lives as well. —1 Thessalonians 2:8*

A Safe Community to Reveal Yourself

Of course, some caution is needed. Some may not understand or value your openness and may spread it like tabloid gossip. Others—reminded of their own pain—may react with sarcasm, anger, or other erratic behavior.

Finding a safe community in which to reveal yourself will be necessary.

Begin with a seasoned counselor. He or she will teach you how to unlock some of those long-closed doors and can show you how sharing such things can still feel safe.

And then find a safe support group. Two keys to look for in such groups: a mature leader who will help protect the safety of what's shared and participants who share your commitment to healing and will protect what is heard.

Opening up to others is risky. But if you trust that God wants to heal you, then trust that He'll make a way for it to happen safely and securely.

As iron sharpens iron, so one person sharpens another.
—Proverbs 27:17

An Accepting Community to Reveal Yourself

Another requirement for safe community is acceptance. Most won't open up for fear of rejection. Won't others turn their heads in disgust when you reveal your wounds? Won't they ask you to find someplace else where people actually want to hear such uncomfortable details?

Sadly, some gatherings are like this. Certain support groups are really social clubs in disguise or groups that want to be educated on healing but don't really want to wade through the messiness of shame and pain. Safe groups are out there, but test the waters before you let down your guard.

A safe group will have the look of hopeful brokenness. When you reveal your wounds, eyes will light up in recognition, and hearts will beam with compassion. You'll be wrapped in acceptance. Your wrongs may not feel right, but finally you'll be among those who understand and want to help bear your burden toward healing.

Find communities that have themselves found acceptance. Those are the ones that will pass on to you what they've so gratefully received.

Accept one another, then, just as Christ accepted you. —Romans 15:7

Being open to Feedback

Have you ever seen your image in a mirror and then shortly after looked at a recent photo of yourself and gasped? How could you look so different?

What about when you speak? Most people grow accustomed to the way they sound. But then you record your voice and play it back. That can't be you, can it?

The way we see ourselves in photos or hear ourselves on recordings is how others see and hear us. But we can't see that from our own perspective. We need to step outside ourselves to get a better understanding of who we are.

We waste a lot of time arguing with others about how we come across. But we're using different filters, and we need to respect the feedback we get in our safe communities when others point out something we may not recognize or accept about ourselves.

Want to discover more about who you are? Then listen to what others tell you.

Those who disregard discipline despise themselves, but the one who heeds correction gains understanding. —Proverbs 15:32

To Live and Move and Have Your Being

Here's a fact that may free you to live a life of openness: no one can judge you more than God.

We fear the judgment of others, but consider how meaningless those judgments are. In seeking God's forgiveness, you'll discover that these other humans are just guessing. Only God really knows you through and through. And through His forgiveness, you'll find love and acceptance despite His judgments. When you discover similar acceptance in safe communities, the judgments of others will lose their power.

It's not that your wounds are gone or that you have no more healing to do. It's that you'll finally be comfortable in your own shoes—in both your pain and your immense value to those who matter to you.

Your openness will be a sign that the shackles of pain are crumbling and that you can finally live and move and have your being in the life that matters.

"If the Son sets you free, you will be free indeed." —John 8:36

The Language of Communion

How well we communicate matters in virtually every area of life and could have been addressed in every section of this book. But most of the words of Scripture are about what's wrong and about how to make it right. So communication is probably best addressed here.

It is no accident that the word *communicate* sounds similar to the words *community* and *communion*. Words are the primary way to connect, or reconnect, to what matters, particularly our relationships with God, others, and ourselves.

One of the chief vehicles for your journey toward wholeness and reconnection will be how much you value the words you use, how much you understand their meaning and power, and how much you're up for the task of learning a new language.

Embrace the glorious and beautiful language of communion.

The unfolding of your words gives light; it gives understanding to the simple. —Psalm 119:130

The Power of Words

Words have power. From your earliest years, you discovered this. Your parents delighted when you spoke for the first time. Sometimes it took just one word to get what you wanted, whether it was food or affection.

Words shape your world. Words spoken and heard both tickle your fancy and add color and beauty. They invite you to discover all that is yet unnamed and undefined.

Words bind one to another in relationship. Words of greeting begin friendships. Words of love launch new romances. Words invite your children to know their world like you grew to know yours. They are the very fabric of personal connection.

Words create and destroy. Words have built you up, and words have been your undoing. You've lifted others up and with your words, and you've torn others down.

Consider the power of words. Power should be respected and celebrated, and it should not be used lightly.

The tongue has the power of life and death, and those who love it will eat its fruit. —Proverbs 18:21

His Words

His words matter. They are God's intimate communication with us and for us.

His words are not simply a dry, ancient set of rules sent to place us under a condemning eye. His words are living. They're the very essence of God Himself, the source of life. His words are personal. His Word is a person—Jesus, the Son of God.

His words are as complex, simple, encouraging, mysterious, and convicting as any fully drawn person would be. His words speak to our deepest needs. They understand our weaknesses and call us to know God's strengths.

His words declare what's wrong—all the weakness, violence, and despair. But His words also point us to how to make it right—calling us out of our self-destruction and into a new dawn of joy and rest.

As God's communication to man, His words connect to us on every level, just as God Himself does.

In the beginning was the Word, and the Word was with God, and the Word was God. . . . In him was life, and that life was the light of all mankind. —John 1:1, 4

Learning a New Language

Do you speak *God*?

If you want to become more fluent in making what's wrong right again, you need to learn how to speak His language.

Start with some vocabulary. *Love*, for instance. Is it possible that God's definition is different than yours? How about words like *peace*, *joy*, *sin*, or *hatred*? To learn God's language, you shouldn't take for granted that your vocabulary is God's vocabulary.

Learn His rules of grammar, the appropriate use and structure of God's words. Perhaps you've defined God's love, but can you communicate it properly in a relationship? Or the rules of syntax, how God's words relate to each other. Can you translate how God's peace relates to your daily life? Learn how to put that relationship into words.

To communicate what matters, you need to make the assumption that you've never really spoken before. Walk in the humility of a child, learning for the first time the ABCs of God's communication.

> *"As the heavens are higher than the earth, so are my ways higher than your ways and my thoughts than your thoughts."* —Isaiah 55:9

Words That Reflect

As communicators, we often deliver speeches when we think we're engaged in conversation. When someone does speak, we're just formulating our response. Our words are not about connection. They're about us.

But your words should always be about connection. Even when you keep a journal or speak to yourself in solitude, there's still someone addressed—yourself. Your words should connect you to who you are as well as connect you to others.

For this to happen, your words should reflect. You should read God's words and let your words reflect His. In communicating with others, your words still should reflect. You can share the loftiest words imaginable—*love, peace, joy*—but if those words aren't a reflection of the listener's needs, understanding, or ways of speaking, then you might as well be speaking to a brick wall.

Communication should be communal.

Everyone should be quick to listen, slow to speak and slow to become angry. —James 1:19

Words of Life

What's wrong with our words?

Our words have become empty. We speak more slang than substance. Our profanities aren't just offensive to grandmothers and church ladies; they describe our lowest animal instincts.

Our words have become hurtful. We gossip about others when they're not around. We speak with sarcasm, disrespect, or indifference when they are. However subtle, our speech raises us up and puts others down.

If you're yearning for what's wrong to be made right, start with your words. Are they lazy and empty, or are they intentional and full of meaning? Are they a thinly veiled strategy to pat yourself on the back while throwing others under the bus? Or are they words that reflect, words that seek to honor and respect others, whether they're in your presence or not?

Words were the first source of life itself. Communicate words of life.

Do not let any unwholesome talk come out of your mouths, but only what is helpful for building others up according to their needs, that it may benefit those who listen. —Ephesians 4:29

The Right Words in a Wrong World

What's wrong can be made right again. But what's right has never been absent.

It can be found in the quiet words of a counselor to someone racked with guilt and shame. Or when a bullied child is praised by his teacher for his work on a class project. Or when you're about to give up but hear the words from above: *I'm not done with you yet.*

What is the communication of your life? Is it that because there's so much wrong with the world, there's no use in trying? That we should all just look out for number one? If so, you'll have little problem communicating with others who speak the same language. Your words won't matter.

No matter how wrong the world is, the right words have been spoken from the beginning. They're near you. Perhaps they're even on the tip of your tongue. So try it. Speak the right words, and watch how they will change your world.

The word is very near you; it is in your mouth and in your heart so you may obey it. —Deuteronomy 30:14

Practicing the Principle of Presence

In the movie *Harvey*, Elwood P. Dowd is a man whose family tries to commit him to a mental asylum for believing in a large, invisible rabbit.

But Elwood proves to be saner than anyone. That's because despite his odd ways, he understands the principle of *presence*. No matter who he meets, that person is the most important person in the world. He puts people at ease, makes them feel important, and invites virtually everyone over for dinner.

Most people live life somewhere else. The past. The future. They're distracted by paying bills, or measuring up, or fitting in. So it's no wonder that other people are mere objects to be ignored or obstacles they trip over on their way to nowhere.

The life that matters is lived in no other place than here. Now. With you. Practice the principle of presence, and let the rest of the world live in the asylum.

"Therefore do not worry about tomorrow, for tomorrow will worry about itself." —Matthew 6:34

There You Are!

It's been said that there are two kinds of people: *Here I am!* people and *There you are!* people.

The *Here I am!* people are usually outgoing and fun to be around. But really they're about calling attention to themselves and have little interest in noticing others. Those around them are an audience and little more.

The *There You Are!* people, however, call attention to you. They greet you like they haven't seen you in years. They lift your spirits with their warmth and interest. It's clear that there's no other place they would rather be than there with you.

The first step to being present with people is admitting whether your first instinct is to notice others or—in your outgoing or even shy ways—to prefer that they notice you. Real presence is found in putting others first on your radar and reminding them that they matter.

I have much to write to you, but I do not want to use paper and ink. Instead, I hope to visit you and talk with you face to face.
—2 John 1:12

Target Practice

Perhaps you're thinking that being present may come naturally to some but that it's just not in your personality. You're either too high-strung or too shy to zero in on others that way.

One, realize that you're never going to be present in the exact way others will. And that's okay. Two, if it matters that everyone is present, then there will be a way for you to do it too.

It's a little like target practice. No one starts out hitting the bull's-eye every time. They have to practice. They have to stop, focus on their target, and shoot. Will people miss? Of course, but the more they shoot, the more they'll hit the target.

Simply remind yourself that most everyone you run into is more important than where you're headed or what's on your mind. Stop, focus, and shoot. Eventually, what begins as a discipline will come easily.

Do not forget to show hospitality to strangers, for by so doing some people have shown hospitality to angels without knowing it.
—Hebrews 13:2

Questions and Answers

There are two types of people when you're out to eat: those who dominate the conversation and those who speak only when spoken to. Well really, there's a third, which is who you want to be: the person who is about *questions* and *answers*.

At a restaurant—or anywhere for that matter—show others their importance by treating them like the subject of an important news story. Rather than just talking about yourself or waiting for them to engage you, take the initiative and start asking questions.

Questions like, "So what's new in your world?" Or, "Tell me about the family. Any updates on the kids?" And then when they speak, listen to their answers. Their answers will probably inspire more questions, and *voila!* You've just whipped up some presence.

If you're new to this kind of thing, remember: most people love to talk about themselves. Your job is to just get them started.

Everyone should be quick to listen, slow to speak and slow to become angry. —James 1:19

What They Need Most

Presence always matters, but it may matter most when everything right has all gone wrong. Someone is grieving a death. Or suffering from a serious illness. Or depressed, angry, or discouraged.

At these times, the best way to be present with someone is usually to just be present. Nothing more. No friendly banter. No advice. No praise or encouragement. No drawn-out words of comfort. Just you, with them. And that's it.

Let them talk if they want to talk. Or hold them as they cry. Or maybe they'll just want to be silent. The silence may feel uncomfortable. Just sitting there will feel impractical. But it's not.

We want to help. That's why we're there. But when people are at their worst, don't ask what you can do for them. They probably don't need favors or errands. They don't even need your words. What do they need most? You.

Just you.

Our hope for you is firm, because we know that just as you share in our sufferings, so also you share in our comfort.
—*2 Corinthians 1:7*

The Master of Presence

Jesus practiced presence.

He looked into the heart of need and met people there. Social outcasts. Prostitutes. Tax collectors. Victims of disease or spiritual anguish. Blue-collar workers. Grieving parents. Religious authorities. Military men. Whoever they were, whatever their state in life, He encountered them, looked them in the eye, and told them once and for all that they mattered.

You're not Jesus, but if you ask Him, He'll likely give you the guidance you need when you encounter people at this level. Who are they? What's in their heart? What do they need most? Warm conversation? A hug? A listening ear? A swift kick in the pants? You're not a mind reader, but Jesus is. Ask Him. Then put on your x-ray glasses to see what you can see.

Hopefully Jesus has encountered you too. If you want to get better at being present with others, consider being more present with Him.

The Samaritan woman said to him, "You are a Jew and I am a Samaritan woman. How can you ask me for a drink?" (For Jews do not associate with Samaritans.) —John 4:9

Who Is Your Neighbor?

Mr. Rogers was long known for his children's show on public television. He had a soft, lilting voice as he spoke to his youngest viewers, and this led to frequent mockery by comedians.

But what seemed a childlike speaking style had everything to do with presence. He looked intently into the camera as if a single child were right in front of him. He told kids that they were special just as they were.

He addressed every area of their need—from imagination to anger to divorce. He invited them to be his neighbor. Despite his audience, it's clear that Mr. Rogers's skill for presence could be modeled for any age.

Who are your neighbors? Really, it's anyone who is near. There's too much wrong in the world for you to just pass them by. You can—as Fred Rogers once said—love them into being. Stop and smell this fragrant presence of humanity. You can be their neighbor.

So he asked Jesus, "And who is my neighbor?" . . . The expert in the law replied, "The one who had mercy on him."
   Jesus told him, "Go and do likewise." —Luke 10:29, 37

Hope for a New World

For the wrongs in your world to be made right, you have to believe in hope.

Otherwise, what's wrong is just wrong. And if that's the case, nothing really matters. But despite the pain it inflicts, what's wrong can still find its purpose if it's eventually going to be made right. That needs to be your hope.

But when? *When* will all your wrongs be made right? In some cases, not until your next life begins. But your present days can still sustain you and spur you toward the finish line.

One day, there'll be a new world where all wrongs are right. No more pain or death. We'll live in eternal presence with others. No matter how wrong things are in the world you know, hope can carry you on to that brand-new day.

"Blessed are the poor in spirit, for theirs is the kingdom of heaven."
—*Matthew 5:3*

Hope for a Release from Pain

The best way to confront your pain is to remember that one day it will be no more.

Whether it's the pain of physical sickness, emotional wounds, or grief, it's a tall order to face your pain and seek healing or wholeness. You've gained some tools to climb that mountain, but the best equipment doesn't make the mountain any less steep or challenging to climb.

So while you address your pain, embrace the comfort of God and others who will enter into your suffering and help you bear these burdens. They may not remove the pain or the source that caused it, but they will remind you that you matter, and that will sustain you to climb again.

The comfort you receive will give you hope for the final comfort, when there will be a release from all pain.

"Blessed are those who mourn, for they will be comforted."
—*Matthew 5:4*

Hope for a Sense of Place

Do you have a sense of place?

Of course, you live somewhere. But do you *live* where you live? Or is it just four walls and an electric bill? Your sense of place is more than just your living quarters. It's where you belong. It's where life most matters.

People who don't have that find themselves constantly driven. Whether it's in their work, their studies, or the way they relate to others, they're always searching for something—often something they can't define. They feel like it's up to them to find it. What they never find is peace.

Realize that your greatest sense of place and peace isn't in a location; it's in a people. You probably already know this when it comes to family. But mostly it's in one person: God. He is your ultimate sense of place, and your hope should be in Him.

Plant your roots in God, and He will give you a place to hang your hat until the day you can set up residence in His house permanently.

"Blessed are the meek, for they will inherit the earth."
—Matthew 5:5

Hope for a Sense of Fulfillment

Don't fill up on bread! Remember hearing that from your parents? No matter how good the bread tasted, the main course would be so much better. It was important to stay hungry for what was coming.

Like waiting all day to eat at your favorite restaurant, we're all hungering and thirsting for fulfillment. Too often, we jump in and eat the first thing put in front of us and have no room for what God wants to feed us.

By letting God feed you with His right thinking and stepping out to live for what is right, you'll find the fulfillment that bread alone could never provide.

Hope for the day when you'll hunger and thirst no more. And in the meantime, stay hungry.

"Blessed are those who hunger and thirst for righteousness, for they will be filled." —Matthew 5:6

Hope for a New Start

Everyone likes the idea of a do-over. Perhaps that's why reincarnation is such an attractive belief. When we look at all the wrong in the world—some of it caused by us—it's a relief to think that we could get another chance to start over again after we die.

But the Bible makes it clear that this life is our only earthly shot. That certainly ups the ante. Still, this life is jam-packed with do-overs if you're willing to take advantage of them.

Do-overs with God are available through His mercy. He doesn't have to let us off the hook, but He does. If we have no hope for God's mercy, we'll never forgive ourselves, and we'll certainly never forgive others.

But we still mess up. Others still hurt us. And so the mercy cycle must continue. We can rest in the hope that through the work of God's Son, everyone who wants it will have an eternal do-over, a new start that will last forever.

"Blessed are the merciful, for they will be shown mercy."
—*Matthew 5:7*

Hope for a New Vision

People who need glasses don't always realize they need glasses. But then one day they go in for a routine eye exam and are told that their vision is impaired. They don't see as well as they thought they did.

Then they put on glasses and see the difference. They never realized how much they were straining to see. The world is so much clearer!

Shifting your focus to hope for what is right is like putting on new glasses. Hope can purify the cynicism in your bones and help you see that not *everything* around you is going to hell in a handbasket. It can reveal light in the world that you may have missed. It can show you the source of that light—God Himself.

If all you see in the world is what's wrong with it, consider the possibility that your vision isn't is great as you think it is. Try on the glasses of hope, and you'll be amazed by what you see.

"Blessed are the pure in heart, for they will see God."
—Matthew 5:8

Hope for a New You

Did you know that Jesus isn't the only Son of God? The first man, Adam, was called God's son. And Eve was His daughter. There was a time when men and women were children of God and everything in the world was right.

But now so much is wrong. The wrong is so much easier to spot than what is right, it makes us want to give up. Or protest. Or rebel. Or cry out in pain. How could so much go wrong? What's the point of even entertaining what is right in a world gone so wrong?

The supreme Son of God, Jesus, came to offer you the opportunity to make peace with God, with others, and with yourself. If you live in that kind of peace, perhaps you can make peace with the wrong you see as well. As a son or daughter of God, you now have a hope that what was wrong can be made right again.

And that's a hope worth living for.

"Blessed are the peacemakers, for they will be called children of God." —Matthew 5:9

PART 6:

HOW TO BECOME A BETTER HUMAN BEING

Considering Your Character

In most stories, the main characters will undergo change. They start out as they are . . . then something happens. They're sent off on an adventure, trouble drops on their doorstep, or some challenge must be overcome. As they seek to overcome the challenge or banish the trouble, they begin to change. At the end of the story, they are usually different people altogether.

While you aren't the main character in God's story, you are the main character in yours. If you've read this far, hopefully you've felt the call to adventure. Perhaps, you've seen that some trouble needs addressing, some challenges need to be overcome.

If so, expect that in living a story that matters, your character will undergo some change. Some of it will just happen. Your role in the change is actually a big part of the story itself.

Who you're becoming matters, and that starts with considering your character.

Not only so, but we also glory in our sufferings, because we know that suffering produces perseverance; perseverance, character; and character, hope. —Romans 5:3–4

Make Sure Your Matter Matters

The word *matter* is used a lot in this book. But it's used in other areas of thought as well.

In science, matter is anything that's physical, anything that takes up space. Scientists and engineers admire matter that has integrity, matter with a structural makeup that is solid. When matter doesn't have that kind of integrity, it's considered unstable, like a condemned building or an explosive chemical.

For your character to matter, you also need to have integrity. Your substance needs to be consistent and solid through and through. Who you appear to be in public should essentially be who you are in private. What you say should be consistent with what is true or honest. When you make a promise, you should actually deliver.

Not only do you matter, but you actually *are* matter! For your matter to matter, you need to pursue a life of integrity.

The integrity of the upright guides them, but the unfaithful are destroyed by their duplicity. —Proverbs 11:3

The Buck Begins Here

President Harry S. Truman had a sign on his desk that read, The Buck Stops Here. This referred to another phrase, *passing the buck*, which meant avoiding responsibility for your actions. Truman was taking responsibility for his.

As you start out on the road toward character change, you'll notice some resistance. Most often, that resistance will come from you.

One way to recognize this resistance is to admit how often you pass the buck. When something needs doing, do you do it yourself, or do you always expect others to do it for you? When something goes wrong, do you immediately take ownership for your role, or do you blame everyone else? These are warning signs that you're probably not ready for change.

A person of character is one who not only accepts responsibility but looks for it. So if you want to pursue the change that matters, the buck shouldn't just stop here; the buck should *begin* here.

For each one should carry their own load. —Galatians 6:5

The Source Underneath

Clean water is a real need in third-world countries. Families draw their water from contaminated rivers and often contract disease trying to meet their most basic needs. One of the best solutions has been to dig new wells. Often, beneath their very feet is a source of pure water. They just need the means to get to it and bring it to the surface.

We often draw from contaminated water when it comes to our character. We need love but are poisoned by dysfunction and hurt. We long for peace but end up with numbed forgetfulness. We thirst for joy but drink empty pleasure and distraction.

If you've turned your life over to God, His Spirit comes to live within you. There's a source of pure water underneath that you can draw from. You'll need some tools to bring it to the surface—prayer, Bible reading, worship.

But you no longer have to draw from the contaminated rivers of the world.

Create in me a pure heart, O God, and renew a steadfast spirit within me. —Psalm 51:10

A Beautiful Character

There's a saying that what is beautiful isn't always good but that what is good is always beautiful.

The first part is true in the world of entertainment. If a TV show or movie is beautiful—the look, feel, and storytelling evokes pleasure or excitement—then we are told it must also be good, even if it isn't.

But consider the second part. If a man, just out of jail, wears thrift store clothes to apply for work and live responsibly, that's beautiful. If a woman dresses more modestly to honor her purity and not tempt her male coworkers, that's also beautiful. These good acts may not be beautiful in our culture's eyes, but in the life that matters, they are drop-dead gorgeous.

Don't look to our culture to define how you should look to others. Honor God and others with your good character, and your show will be must-see viewing.

Charm is deceptive, and beauty is fleeting; but a woman who fears the LORD is to be praised. —*Proverbs 31:30*

When Life Isn't Fair

We grow up learning that life isn't always fair. The rich get richer. Pretty girls get the guy. Bad people get away. You just can't find an honest mechanic. While some of these complaints may not be as true as we imagine, it is true that life isn't always fair.

But does this excuse you to respond in kind? If a mechanic cheats you, does that mean you should take advantage of others? Because some pretty girl stole your guy in high school, does that mean you should punish your husband for not meeting your teenage fantasy? Because people hurt others and get away with it, does that mean you shouldn't come clean when you realize you've caused someone pain?

The life that matters is often what you make it. Let your character ring true in how you treat others. The fairer you are, the more the unfairness around you won't matter.

What does the LORD require of you? To act justly and to love mercy and to walk humbly with your God. —Micah 6:8

Gold-Plated Gold

Some people enjoy wearing costume jewelry. It's inexpensive and it looks like the real thing. A gold-plated necklace to the casual observer looks like a necklace of the purest gold.

When it comes to character, we can look like costume jewelry. We may be tarnished brass on the inside, but what others see has the appearance of gold. There are parts of our character where we put on a costume to look honorable, but it's not who we really are.

Allow God to change these areas, and you'll notice a difference. The gold won't be just on the outside but will show up on the inside too. You won't have the appearance of honor. You will actually think and act honorably.

Your character will finally match the priceless value God has seen in you all along. You'll be a bit of pure gold, and the costumes you wear will no longer be necessary.

A good character is the best tombstone. Those who loved you and were helped by you will remember you. Carve your name on hearts, not on marble. —Charles Spurgeon

Your Job Description

Becoming a better human being means making better choices. This may seem like a tall order. Isn't it impossible to know where your choices will lead? Aren't there myriad variables we can't control so that our choices are like creating a small ripple in a vast ocean? How can our choices really matter?

While some of those concerns are valid, they don't excuse not pursuing a life of self-control. First, if you don't really know where your choices will lead, isn't it possible that they could have a much greater impact than you imagine?

Second, while there is a great deal out there you can't control, that's God's job. Your job description is to make your choices matter by trusting Him, and making sure your choices, large and small, will honor Him.

Take back control over the choices you make, and leave the rest of the ocean to Him.

It is God who works in you to will and to act in order to fulfill his good purpose. —Philippians 2:13

Life on Spin Cycle

You seriously had the best intentions. You tried to make the right choice. But then (*choose which one applies*)—life threw you a curve ball; you were in the wrong place at the wrong time; you couldn't help it; other people didn't want you to succeed.

Whatever the circumstances, whatever you intended to do, you didn't end up doing it. Unless something changes, it's likely you'll find yourself there again and again.

In the same way your washer's spin cycle drains water from your clothes, so will an endless cycle of good intentions and bad choices drain you of any hope that your life will matter.

You can't take your life off spin cycle, but there's someone who can. Your most important choice will be whether you will follow His guidance in every way.

I have the desire to do what is good, but I cannot carry it out. For what I do not do the good I want to do, but the evil I do not want to do—this I keep on doing. —Romans 7:18–19

The Better Gamble

Imagine your favorite meal. Now imagine it sitting before you, just waiting to be eaten. But there's a catch. Somewhere within this greatest of meals is a small bit of poison. Not a lot. It might not even kill you. Would you still eat it?

Most people would say no. It's not a worthwhile risk! Others might be cautious—but then decide that the payoff is worth the risk.

Whether it's romantic relationships, money decisions, or what we put in our bodies, our choices can too often demonstrate that we care more about our pleasure than our consequences.

If you're a risk-taker, consider the gamble of choosing God's guidance regarding your choices. He's prepared a meal that is far more pleasurable than any earthly thing you can imagine. The only thing hidden inside is a life that matters.

> *Belief is a wise wager. . . . If you gain, you gain all; if you lose, you lose nothing. Wager, then, without hesitation, that He exists.*
> *—Blaise Pascal*

Becoming a Student of Good Choices

If you've decided to seek God's guidance in making better choices, where do you start?

The first place you need to start is in prayer. If you've been alive for very long, some patterns of poor decision-making will be hard to break. Start by praying for a true *desire* to make different choices. We often imagine we have the desire, but many of us don't.

Then look to God's textbook, the Bible, for good choices. As you read God's will for your choices, you'll not just start building a mental inventory on what to do, but God's Spirit will move your heart to actually do it.

A good student always communicates with the teacher. A good student will read the assigned textbook for the class. Decide that passing God's class is in your best interests, and you'll be on the road to making better choices.

I will instruct you and teach you in the way you should go; I will counsel you with my loving eye on you. —Psalm 32:8

Reaction Versus Proaction

As you look to God more and more for guidance in your choices, it's still possible to find your life on spin cycle. You wake up, perhaps mutter a brief prayer, but still behave the exact opposite way you intended. This is probably because you're spending more time reacting than being proactive.

Wake up in the morning with a game plan in mind. Have problems getting along with others? Plan to offer them kindness before they have a chance to annoy you. Make too many impulse purchases? Write out a budget and wake up knowing exactly how much you have to spend that day. Overeat when you're stressed? Plan moments of peace throughout your day, and plan a daily calorie limit you'll stick to.

You can't run the world, but you also don't have to let the world run you. Plan ahead. Stick to your plan. And your good intentions can match your actions.

"Suppose one of you wants to build a tower. Won't you first sit down and estimate the cost to see if you have enough money to complete it?" —Luke 14:28

What Choice Do You Have?

Just as there is opportunity in trouble, there is also opportunity in every choice. On the downside, you can also choose to make things worse. And very often, one bad choice leads to another.

But even when you find yourself in the pit of bad choices, there is no point at which you can't start making good choices. Every good choice is an opportunity to discover more good choices just ripe for the picking.

So what matters here is how you see your choices. Do you just choose without thinking? That's a wasted choice. Do you choose in a state of hopelessness, assuming that whatever you choose, your life will remain a mess? That's also a waste. Do you feel like you really have no choice? Waste, waste, waste.

What choice do you have? You have the next choice. And from there, a multitude of good or bad choices awaits you. Use your freedom to choose wisely.

Live as free people, but do not use your freedom as a cover-up for evil; live as God's slaves. —1 Peter 2:16

Moving from Good to Best

People who have learned the habit of making good choices may feel satisfied that their work is done. But the life that matters requires a higher standard.

Perhaps you feel you're doing well in not responding in anger when you used to always lose your cool. However, what's best is not just keeping your cool, but also being the first to offer a kindness or admit you're wrong. Maybe you're now making good money choices and not buying what you want when you want it. What's best is not just stopping unwise spending, but starting a savings account and giving more to charity.

Moving from good to best in your choices is where you should be headed. It's also the way to safeguard your choices from ever becoming bad choices again. While it is not always the easiest path to walk, it does make it more possible to live the life that matters.

"I have the right to do anything," you say—but not everything is beneficial. —1 Corinthians 6:12

Whatever It Takes

What do you want? Some people never ask this question, but hopefully you have by now.

Another question: *If what you want matters, what are you willing to sacrifice to get it?* This one is often a deal-breaker. Many want a life that matters, but they don't want to put in the hard work it takes to attain it.

But if you want to become a better human being, that kind of discipline is non-negotiable. Nothing worth having comes easy. Even the most satisfying sleep and peace are usually won through a day's hard work of intentional living.

Whether it's improving your character, making better choices, or achieving a better life, the goal has to be worth the sacrifice, or you'll never put in the effort and endure the pain to reach it.

Becoming a better human being matters. What are you willing to do to get there?

Commit to the Lord whatever you do, and he will establish your plans. —Proverbs 16:3

Surrender to the Authorities

In setting out to become a better person, your daily focus shouldn't be *change*; it should be *surrender*.

Let's say you want to get back in shape by running a 5K. When you wake up, your first thoughts probably aren't about standing at the finish line. You're thinking that you don't want to get out of bed. Or how hard it will be to find your running shoes. Or whether you can make it the first mile. Essentially, you have to surrender your desire to stay under the covers because running is more important than sleeping in.

Discipline is about surrendering to the authorities—the fitness experts who tell you what it takes to complete a 5K, and to God, who is the best authority on what it takes to become a better human being.

As much as the goal is *why* you run the race, discipline and surrender are the *how*. Trust that the authorities know what they're talking about, and you'll find yourself changing before you know it.

Offer your bodies as a living sacrifice. . . . Be transformed by the renewing of your mind. —Romans 12:1–2

Theory for Practice, Excuses for Action

A professor was once asked whether, given the choice, he would rather hear a lecture about heaven or actually go to heaven. He chose the lecture. We too love talking about becoming better human beings, but when it comes to actually doing it, we're far more interested in theory than we are in practice.

We also love to entertain our excuses. Change means giving up what's familiar to step into the unknown. And that scares us. We're afraid of the unknown. We're certainly afraid of failure. So we come up with a mile-long list of excuses that keep us from acting.

One of your first disciplines must be to surrender your theory for practice, your excuses for action. You must push through your fear of the unknown, the discomfort of change, the pain of failure, knowing that—compared with the goal you're striving for—they don't really matter.

Do not merely listen to the word, and so deceive yourselves. Do what it says. —James 1:22

Your Itinerary for Change

People have different ideas about what makes for a good vacation. If touring Europe, some would just want to get off the plane and let life take its course. Finding a place to stay and the sites, cities, or countries they would discover would be left to adventurous chance.

Others would plan their trip. They'd research where to stay and go, and then they'd stick to a daily itinerary. In this way, they could enjoy the trip by not missing out on the best destinations.

While both philosophies have merit, your trip to becoming a better human being will require some organization. You'll need to research and get good advice on the best places to go. You'll need to map out your path and order your steps. Then you'll need discipline to stick to your travel plans.

By setting an itinerary for change, you'll be able to mark your progress and you won't find yourself lost along the way.

Give careful thought to the paths for your feet and be steadfast in all your ways. —Proverbs 4:26

The Importance of Repetition

How do you practice a discipline? Over and over and over.

We've been fooled into thinking that what matters is only what's new, what's exciting, or what entertains. So the mundane, boring periods of life become the waiting room we endure until we can do something more exciting.

But look at people you admire. Elite basketball players. Brilliant scientists. They didn't get where they are by waiting to be entertained. Their greatness was won in the unseen backrooms of repeated, boring discipline. Running sprints and shooting drills. Methodical observation and repeated experimentation.

Becoming a better human being requires settling into a daily routine of seeking God and His guidance, practicing what you learn, and starting over tomorrow to do it all again. This is where returning to the same scriptures over and over is necessary. Just because you understand a life principle doesn't mean you'll actually live it. You'll only live it if it becomes part of you, and that requires repetition.

I have hidden your word in my heart that I might not sin against you. —Psalm 119:11

Improvise, Adapt, and Overcome

The Marines are famous for their discipline. They train through repetition. They have a whatever-it-takes attitude. They submit to authority and stick to set rules of engagement. But the Marines are also used in difficult warfare situations because of their ability to improvise, adapt, and overcome.

Battles often go in a different direction than expected. Some challenges require shifting quickly from one approach to the next. It's at those times that Marines must use their training and discipline to overcome these life-and-death challenges.

You can't tackle the challenge of becoming a better person without a good deal of discipline under your belt. Sometimes your best discipline will be knowing when your current method of change isn't working and adapting to a different approach.

Like the Marines, remain always faithful to the mission of change, and you'll find you can overcome just about anything.

I have become all things to all people so that by all possible means I might save some. I do all this for the sake of the gospel, that I may share in its blessings. —1 Corinthians 9:22–23

The Reason You Sacrifice

No matter how much discipline you have, at some point, you're going to run out of steam. You decide the goal isn't worth the sacrifice because, frankly, you don't feel you're worth the effort.

But then you remember: the life that matters is not just about you. In the same light, *you* are not just about you. You are meant for more than yourself.

There's your motivation. You discipline yourself so that others will benefit from your existence on this planet. They will benefit from your good character and your good choices. They will want to be better people because of your example. Life generates more life.

What do you want? Will you do whatever it takes to get it? Those who matter to you can become better human beings too if you discipline yourself to make it happen.

"For them I sanctify myself, that they too may be truly sanctified."
—John 17:19

Making Your Consumption Matter

Food is a very emotional topic for many. Some love to lecture people on eating healthy. Others just want to eat what they like and enjoy life. What you consume matters in both practical and eternal ways.

While not all sickness can be avoided, it can certainly be slowed and minimized through your lifestyle and what you put into your body. Of course, this includes nicotine, alcohol, and other substances, but food alone is worthy of discussion since everyone on the planet eats.

It's not about removing the joy from eating. It's about making your consumption matter. Becoming a better person will be far more challenging if your body isn't in good enough shape to take you there.

So start making better choices about what you consume. You'll improve your odds of living the life that matters.

Dear friend, I pray that you may enjoy good health and that all may go well with you. —3 John 1:2

Your Most Common Reminder

Our hunger for food is a good thing. It's what drives us to survive, to be equipped for whatever life throws at us. It reminds us that life is meant to be savored and enjoyed.

But it can also be a source of stress. When we're hungry, we feel weak. We lose focus. When we're overweight or sick due to our eating habits, hunger may bring more sorrow than happiness.

The best way to find balance with your hunger is to remember that everything God created points back to Him. Hunger is your most common reminder that you can't go a day without being in need. And what could you possibly need more than God?

Use your hunger as a way to feed on what you really need, and you'll find less stress and more joy in the food that's on your plate.

"I have food to eat that you know nothing about." . . . "My food," said Jesus, "is to do the will of him who sent me and to finish his work." —John 4:32, 34

Telling a Cheese Puff from a Carrot

From a distance, you might mistake a cheese puff for a baby carrot. They have a similar color, shape, and size. But looking at the ingredients on their packaging, the cheese puff reads like a chemistry textbook, while the carrot usually just says, *carrots*.

We can be fooled into thinking we're eating what's good for us when it's really not. While processed food tastes great, it's empty of any real substance. It promises pleasure, but it can't deliver good health and longevity. So we need to look at the real ingredients in what we eat in order to become healthier human beings.

The same goes for our spiritual food. We need to listen to God's instruction to tell us what's best there too.

The more you eat what is good—physically and spiritually—the more you'll desire it. You'll hunger for what is good more than what is not.

When the woman saw that the fruit of the tree was good for food and pleasing to the eye, and also desirable for gaining wisdom, she took some and ate it. —Genesis 3:6

Portion Control

In addition to eating healthier, you can still enjoy the foods you like by simply practicing portion control. For some, this requires measuring; for others, it means buying pre-packaged portions. You set a budget for daily intake, and you stick to it.

Portion control teaches you that you don't need as much as you think to live. Also, eating less can be just as satisfying. Your body, your energy level, and your focus will see improvement.

God asked His followers to eat less as a reminder that they should hunger for Him and His guidance as their portion. He wanted us to remember that it's He who truly satisfies, who improves spiritual health, who increases spiritual energy, who gives us spiritual focus and purpose.

Make God your portion and the buffets of the world seem no more than a morsel.

The people shall go out and gather a day's portion every day, that I may test them, whether or not they will walk in My instruction.
—*Exodus 16:4 NASB*

Slow Food

You've probably felt the frustration. The car in front of you in the fast-food line is taking forever! Or you're at a restaurant, you get your food, rush through your meal, and then it's off to who knows where. When we're always in a hurry to eat before moving on to other things, we miss the sense that what we consume should matter.

Perhaps you remember someone in your family baking their own bread. Or making homemade chicken broth. Or that slow-cooker of stew that sat all day, extracting a taste you could never get from a microwave. Food like that shouldn't be disregarded in favor of quick consumption.

The best food or a life-changing idea or the dearest friends are meant to be savored, enjoyed slowly.

Slow down the manner in which you consume things, and the joy of life will last that much longer.

"Slow down. Take a deep breath. What's the hurry? Why wear yourself out? Just what are you after anyway?"
—*Jeremiah 2:25 MSG*

A Balanced Diet

People love trying the next fad diet. They'll give up all fat and eat nothing but salad. They'll swear off sugar and use only chemical-laden substitutes. But your body needs things like fat, carbohydrates, and protein to survive. Rather than eliminating one or more items, what your body really needs is balance.

Sometimes in trying to become better versions of ourselves, we can also go to extremes. Those raised by a strict family may decide that their kids are going to have free rein. A woman abused in past relationships may demand that her husband meet her every need.

But no matter what you've experienced or what you've been told, life is best lived in balance. Kids need both freedom and discipline. Husbands need love and patience just as much as they should give it.

God knows what's good for you. Like eating a balanced diet, make sure you eat everything He puts on your plate.

Balances belong to the LORD; all the weights in the bag are of his making. —Proverbs 16:11

Enjoying the Feast

Becoming a better human being isn't just about portion control and eating your carrots. It's also about feasting and community. There were many feasts throughout the year during Bible times. God knew that part of life's rhythm includes eating a great meal with family and friends. We still do this today around barbecues, birthdays, and holidays.

The occasional feast reminds you that life should be lived to the fullest. This abundance of food and fellowship speaks of the promise that one day the banquet will never end. You'll have all you could ever eat. You'll be eternally healthy and satisfied in communion with God Himself.

But it should also remind you that the world still hungers for this kind of food. So as your mouth waters in anticipation for the next great meal, you should invite others to join you. Together, you'll feast on God's love, His forgiveness, and His guidance on how to live a life that matters.

Together, you will eat and be satisfied.

Do not work for the food which perishes, but for the food which endures to eternal life. —John 6:27 NASB

You Were Made to Move

You are not a lump of clay. From the very moment God breathed into you the breath of life, you became a living being. As a living being, you were made to move.

Your breath is meant to quicken. You're meant to sweat. You're meant to expend energy. You're meant to stretch and grow in strength. You're meant to go somewhere. You're meant to move beyond what you're now capable of doing.

Your movement matters because God believes in action. He moves, acts, and expends His energy on the world with a fierce love for your existence. He wants to move *you* to action, to work out what matters and exercise your reason for being, to strengthen your convictions, to produce a life.

Perhaps you've been still and waiting for life to come to you. Get out of your easy chair. The life that matters is waiting on you to move.

Work out your salvation with fear and trembling, for it is God who works in you to will and to act in order to fulfill his good purpose.
—Philippians 2:12—13

Your First Trip to the Gym

You walk into the gym on your first day, and there they are.

Everyone looks like they belong on TV. Their slim frames and toned muscles. The determined look in their eyes. How can someone run that fast? You could never lift that much weight. You're ready to turn around and go home.

But then you notice the others. An older woman is moving slowly, but she's not stopping. An overweight boy strains on a treadmill, but his dad is nearby, cheering him on. They have the same look in their eyes as the "models." They've come to move, and they won't stop until the workout is done.

Nobody goes from zero to sixty their first time to the gym. Don't compare yourself to others. Just show up and start moving. That look of determination and your resolve to finish what you start is all you really need.

Everyone who competes in the games goes into strict training. They do it to get a crown that will not last, but we do it to get a crown that will last forever. —1 Corinthians 9:25

A Change of Pace

A long with your determination, setting the proper pace for your workouts is key to not giving up.

Start slowly at first. Killing yourself won't accomplish anything. Get the advice of a training coach, and alternate your workout regimen between strength training and cardio. Accomplish small goals in everything you do, and you'll be able to build on that success.

Then, after a while, you'll need to raise the bar. Don't stay satisfied with ten reps when you're able to do twenty. Pick up the pace on the treadmill when the current pace becomes too easy. Over reasonable increments of time, challenge yourself to rise to the next level, to do what you don't think you can do.

Your movement isn't just about getting in shape. It's about making movement a lifestyle. Marathon runners pace themselves to finish the race.

Do you not know that in a race all the runners run, but only one gets the prize? Run in such a way as to get the prize.
—1 Corinthians 9:24

Workout Partners

N o one should move alone.

Okay, sometimes it's just you against the treadmill. But if you're in this for the long haul, remember that your movement shouldn't be detached from the most important thing in life: relationship.

Find a workout partner. She'll call you in the morning to make sure you're up for that day's run. He'll spot you as you strain to raise the weight off your chest one last time, telling you that you can do it. She'll rely on you to do the same, to hold her accountable, to spur her beyond her imagined limitations.

We need others to remind us why moving matters and that our motivation to move isn't just about us. We need physical health so we will be around for those who matter. We need spiritual health so we will be fit for eternity.

The race means a great deal more when someone is running alongside you.

As for Titus, he is my partner and co-worker among you; as for our brothers, they are representatives of the churches and an honor to Christ. —2 Corinthians 8:23

Moving Parts

Eventually, your heart won't be satisfied with the four walls of your workout club. To make movement a lifestyle, you'll need to broaden your horizons around what it means to move.

It's been said that the average stay-at-home parent may walk as many as ten miles a day just taking care of basic necessities. Perhaps it will seem less like work if you consider it part of the movement that matters.

Yard work, riding a bicycle, swimming, walking your dog, hiking on a nearby trail, joining an intramural sports team—these are keys to expanding how you move. Start strengthening every muscle you have, not giving up movement because of pure boredom.

Expanding your movement will expand your understanding about what movement can be. Your body has moving parts that need to be used, and so does life. Exercise your freedom to discover all of life's moving parts.

When I was a child, I talked like a child, I thought like a child, I reasoned like a child. When I became a man, I put the ways of childhood behind me. —1 Corinthians 13:11

Let Yourself Be Moved

The movement that matters is a bit like the chicken and the egg. Do you make the first move? Or are you *moved* to move?

Most things originate from God, and the impulse that gets you off the couch is probably no exception. God works in our hearts to move, but He still allows us to resist that impulse. You don't have to move if you don't want to.

But consider the time when you saw someone in need and were moved to compassion. Remember when you felt that feeling that something was wrong and needed to be addressed? Or when you felt the motivation to stop and savor what matters? God was probably giving you that little nudge, urging you to take one step and then another.

It's up to you to move. But let yourself be moved too. More often than not, it'll send you in a direction that matters.

For prophecy never came by the will of man, but holy men of God spoke as they were moved by the Holy Spirit. —*2 Peter 1:21 NKJV*

Creation's Dance

There's nothing like finishing a great workout. Sweat is pouring. Your breathing slows. You feel like you've left something behind—a bit of weight, a load of anxiety, the fear that you wouldn't finish. It's all gone now, and you feel lighter and stronger for it.

You move throughout your day with a sharpened clarity. You have more energy to engage. You even crave more of what's good for you, like a salad or a tall glass of water. You rest when you need to. But you're already thinking of moving again.

There is a time to stop and notice what matters. But if you don't move, you'll only get to see the tiniest part. Feel the urgings of God to move you toward more. More strength. More wisdom. More flexibility. More life.

Join in the rhythm of creation's dance. Learn the steps to move toward more.

The wise prevail through great power, and those who have knowledge muster their strength. —Proverbs 24:5

The Art of Attitude

There's an easy way to tell whether, at any given time, you believe in what matters.

Your attitude.

Is it negative or positive? Is it rigid or is it flexible? Do you ask yourself, "What's in it for me?" or are you thankful for what you have?

If you really want to become a better human being, you'll need to learn how to master the art of attitude. More than you may like to admit, your thoughts and emotions are yours to control. They're the vehicle that carries you to what matters.

Earlier you were asked: W*hat do you want*? Now the question is: W*hat do you believe?* If you don't believe you can become a better person or that living the life that matters is possible, then your efforts here will be wasted.

Believing isn't always easy. But choosing your attitude can be. And attitude is the gateway to belief.

For as he thinks in his heart, so is he. —Proverbs 23:7 *NKJV*

The Most Precious Gift

Some parents debate whether to let their kids believe in Santa Claus. They don't want to lie to them or set them up for disappointment down the road.

But then they remember when they were kids. Every year, they lived in the starry-eyed hope of magic and wonder. Their belief in Santa had to do with more than just the gifts they received. The joy of believing may have been the most precious gift of all.

Choosing a positive attitude is a little like believing in Santa. You can play the realist and feel comfortable that you'll never be disappointed. Or you can wake up expecting every day to be Christmas. By choosing to believe what your day *could* be, your day may not change, but you will.

Remember the joy, wonder, and anticipation you once had expecting the arrival of that jolly old elf? You can live like that year-round if you choose to believe.

Sin is behovely, but all shall be well and all shall be well and all manner of thing shall be well. —Julian of Norwich

Discovering Your Happiness

If you really believe in what matters, you'll learn to recognize how much is already around you.

We live under the spell of marketing professionals whose job it is to make us feel dissatisfied with our lives. If we can just purchase that one product, they say, we'll finally fill the hole inside. So we want and we crave, but we still feel unhappy, not realizing how happy we should be with what we already have.

And that's discovered through an attitude of thankfulness. Choosing a thankful attitude isn't difficult. You simply need to close your ears to the sirens of discontentment. Then at the top of your lungs, sing the melody of family and friends, the roof over your head, the food in your belly, and the God who loves you.

Make a habit of writing those mental thank-you notes every day, and you'll discover how happy you really are.

Give praise to the LORD, proclaim his name; make known among the nations what he has done. —1 Chronicles 16:8

If You Bend, You Will Not Break

Gumby was a character in children's television from the 1950s onward. Many children, given a Gumby doll, enjoyed stretching his rubber limbs into poses that would send most people to the hospital. This was so common that the name *Gumby* is now interchangeable with the adjective *flexible*.

When it comes to change, most of us aren't that flexible. We want our path to be straightforward, and when something gets in our way, we often demand that the obstacle be removed rather than finding a way around it.

Most of your path to what matters will include steep hills, deep valleys, rocks, and downed trees. It will require you to stop or shift gears, sometimes to turn around or take a different path.

No one expects you to be Gumby, but in flexing your attitude by small degrees, you'll find more and more range to bend in ways you'd have never thought possible.

"But small is the gate and narrow the road that leads to life, and only a few find it." —Matthew 7:14

Willing to Be Ready

A re you ready yet?

He's had a quick shower and is waiting by the door. She's showering, debating over the best outfit, applying makeup, and doing her hair. While his impatience reveals more ignorance than anything, this still illustrates that we have different interpretations of what it means to be ready.

Regardless, it's important to choose an attitude that is ready and willing. Do you walk into work ready and willing to do whatever is asked of you? If your spouse or child comes to you with a request, do you respond with an attitude that doesn't make him or her feel guilty for asking?

Like the example above, people sometimes won't understand what it may take for you to be ready. However, you can still do your part to be ready when the call is made. You have to at least be willing to be ready.

Are you ready yet? The question is more about attitude than anything.

Then I heard the voice of the Lord saying, "Whom shall I send? And who will go for us?" And I said, "Here am I. Send me!"
—Isaiah 6:8

You'll See It in Their Faces

Attitude is usually about other people.

Yes, it's important how you carry yourself in pursuing a life that matters, but it's not just about you. Your attitude sets the stage for how you engage others and usually reveals how important they are in your eyes.

When you approach others, do their faces brighten and relax, or do they frown and grow tense? This may be more about them than you, but if most people seem to respond the same way, you might be considered more of a taker than a giver. Even if you disagree, what matters is the attitude that others perceive.

One attitude borrows from another. Choose to be more positive, more flexible, more willing, and a giving and generous attitude will follow. Determine that others are more important, and you'll see it in their faces when you walk into a room.

"Give, and it will be given to you. A good measure, pressed down, shaken together and running over, will be poured into your lap. For with the measure you use, it will be measured to you." —Luke 6:38

The Same Attitude as Him

When we don't believe in what matters, we live our lives with a bit of a God complex.

We imagine we're all-knowing when we expect life to always disappoint. We have a godlike sense of entitlement when we're not thankful. We assert godlike power when we insist on our own way. We live outside time when we're not ready and willing. We assume a divine right when we take what we believe is ours.

Whether we intend to or not, the image we give off is that the world revolves around us. But God Himself chose a different attitude. He emptied Himself of His divine rights to open up the path to what matters. What right do we have to assume that which God Himself surrendered?

Do you really want to believe in what matters? Then adopt His attitude.

Have the same mindset as Christ Jesus: Who, being in very nature God . . . made himself nothing by taking the very nature of a servant. —Philippians 2:5—7

Ambition Upside Down

Consider revolutionaries such as Galileo, Abraham Lincoln, and Martin Luther King Jr. They saw the world in an entirely different way than the majority. But now most of us look back and realize that they were right. What the world thought was right-side up was actually upside down.

Jesus was a revolutionary in the way He looked at humility. Most people considered humility a virtue, but they tended to relegate it to the harmless domain of kindly grandmothers and reverent monks. People don't believe you can make a difference through humility, but can only leave a mark on the world looking out for number one.

Of course, the desire to make a difference isn't the problem. The problem is that in reaching for the heights of success, we tend to trample on what matters along the way.

Want to be a revolutionary? It may be time to turn your notions of ambition upside down.

"Anyone who wants to be first must be the very last, and the servant of all." —Mark 9:35

Exposing What Is Hidden

Most people agree that pride is a bad thing. We don't like people who are full of themselves, toot their own horns, or step on toes. It's a character trait we'd all like to avoid.

But the real power of pride is in its concealment. In other words, most people who are proud are the last to realize it. We disguise it with terms such as *self-confidence* or *standing our ground*. When someone suggests we might be prideful, we often call them weak or spiteful for thinking it.

Our pride is typically noticeable to others but hidden from us. The way to learn more humility is to place people around you who you trust enough to believe when they call you on it.

Most bad character traits, when exposed to the light, have far less power. Be humble enough to admit that you may be proud in ways you're unable to see.

Do you see a person wise in their own eyes? There is more hope for a fool than for them. —Proverbs 26:12

The Best-Kept Secrets

In your path to more humility, your pride will be exposed, and the good you do should be concealed.

It isn't about rejecting praise for what you do. We all need that kind of encouragement. And it's not about keeping all your good deeds outside the public eye. That's not always possible to accomplish.

It's more about checking your motives when doing a good thing. Ask yourself, "Why am I really doing this?" Even in becoming a better human being, if one of your main motivations is to receive the approval of others, you're doing it for the wrong reasons.

Keeping your good deeds secret is a discipline that will humble you. Your pride will tell you to do otherwise, so you'll have the opportunity to put your pride in its place.

Realize that good deeds have their own reward. More humility is just the icing on the cake.

"But when you give to the needy, do not let your left hand know what your right hand is doing, so that your giving may be in secret."
—*Matthew 6:3–4*

Nothing Is Beneath You

What kind of good deeds should you do? While it is important to have a spirit of service for whatever needs to be done, also seek out deeds that are beneath your status. Only you can decide what those would be.

A great way to learn humility is to make it your goal to serve others in ways you'd never choose, especially when you have "better" things to do, expecting nothing in return.

Too often, when we raise ourselves up through word or deed, we put others down. Acts of humble service bring your pride down to the depths for the purpose of raising others up.

It doesn't mean that you are low and without worth. It means that your purpose is found in elevating what matters. In this way, you will find your sense of self elevated as well.

[A] service that one should perform for another in a Christian community is that of active helpfulness. This means, initially, simple assistance in trifling, external matters. . . . Nobody is too good for the meanest service. —Dietrich Bonhoeffer

It Is to Your Advantage

Some people won't be able to stomach these words on humility, not because they're too proud but because they've been so beaten down by others that the thought of deliberately lowering themselves further makes no sense at all. Won't they make themselves vulnerable to be taken advantage of again?

You may not like the answer: yes and no. Yes, if you seek humility, if you serve others without expecting payment or recognition, you may be taken advantage of.

But also, no. Even if you are taken advantage of, it is ultimately to your advantage: you'll be elevated by a life of purpose. In choosing a lifestyle of lowering yourself for the sake of others, you'll find freedom from the power of hurt and abuse inflicted on you without your permission.

If you've been taken advantage of in the past, choose the path of humility. In this, you can rise again.

"For those who exalt themselves will be humbled, and those who humble themselves will be exalted." —Matthew 23:12

Give Yourself a Time-Out

Children can be terribly impatient. They stomp and cry when they have to wait for anything. Parents will then give them a time-out, teaching them that they don't always get what they want whenever they want it.

While your adult tantrums may be more refined, you may still find yourself no more patient in waiting for the things you want. You might as well be holding your breath for all your anxiety is getting you.

Patience is an act of humility. The world doesn't revolve around you, and you shouldn't expect it to. Even when it comes to your more noble desires, you'll need to give yourself a time-out each time you want the change to come faster than life is bringing it.

We're really no more than children in pursuing the life that matters. So sit down, count to ten, and put a stopper on your hurry to get there.

Be patient and stand firm. —James 5:8

Where Your Confidence Lies

Our culture blames a great deal of our problems on lack of self-esteem. If people had more confidence, it says, they'd all be able to rise higher in life. We even love the phrase, "I can't love others until I learn to love myself."

This is an upside-down way of seeing what matters. While it's certainly true that a strong sense of self-worth is vital for our success and purpose, we'll never get there by just looking inward or by looking out for number one.

To really discover your worth, you need to study and imitate the One who created you. Jesus' confidence was in His Father, and His identity and purpose were defined by His humility and service to others.

Self-esteem is indeed the problem. But the solution is finding your confidence in the most humble Person the world has ever known and then making His image your image.

My hope is built on nothing less than Jesus' blood and righteousness;
I dare not trust the sweetest frame, but wholly lean on Jesus' name.
—Edward Mote

Ladies and Gentlemen

At a performance or speech, audiences are typically addressed as "ladies and gentlemen." When this phrase was first used hundreds of years ago, a *lady* or a *gentleman* was someone from the upper class. But their class wasn't just about money. It represented a world governed by a high sense of taste, courtesy, and good manners.

Today, regardless of class, there are too few ladies and gentlemen. There is rarely a "yes, ma'am" or "yes, sir," a "please" or a "thank you." Few respect others' boundaries. Elders and women aren't honored in the way they deserve. We've lost sight of what it means to make others feel important in the way we treat them.

The best part of what it once meant to be a lady or gentleman is also embodied in what it means to be a better human being. No matter what class you're in, you can still be a person of class. You can show respect for yourself and for others.

Be devoted to one another in love. Honor one another above yourselves. —Romans 12:10

Rituals of Respect

You're at your first gourmet restaurant and can't imagine what all the utensils are for. Then you're told there's a certain order to using them. Why is the napkin folded that way? How many courses are there? You wait patiently, hoping you'll be told what to do.

It seems that everywhere you go, something is expected. Business meetings require a suit and tie. You have to remove your shoes before entering certain homes. Men expect a firm handshake. Your elders prefer formal speech over slang.

It's true that one reason good manners were created was to make the upper class feel important. But the manners that matter are those that make *others*, not you, feel important. So it's wise to honor the rituals of respect, whether you're dining with the queen or in your grandmother's kitchen.

You don't have to become a person of ritual, but loving people well means you will become a person of respect.

We are justified in enforcing good morals, for they belong to all mankind; but we are not justified in enforcing good manners, for good manners always mean our own manners. —G. K. Chesterton

Conversational Courtesies

You've probably heard it said before: *How would you behave if Mother Teresa or Jesus walked into the room?* The goal is to treat everyone with a similar level of respect. And this starts in the area of social interaction and conversation.

How do you greet others? Not everyone expects a formal greeting, but some do. Do them the honor of remembering and repeating their name. Show your attentiveness and interest, no matter the topic. Try to make your tone as friendly as possible. Where appropriate, compliment them on their attire or some known accomplishment.

The courtesy you show isn't about trying to impress or behaving falsely. It's about leaving a legacy for what matters every time you engage another human. We are all precious and deserving of kindness, but we are reminded of this all too rarely. With your simple acts of courtesy, you can give the gift of that reminder.

Gracious words are a honeycomb, sweet to the soul and healing to the bones. —Proverbs 16:24

Watch Your Bearing

Another way to improve your manners is in your *bearing*—how you carry yourself and come across to others.

Start with dress and hygiene. Everyone should honor themselves and others through modest attire. Remember that cleanliness isn't just about your health but about respecting the sensitivities of those around you.

How are your boundaries? Your neighbors may like cats, but they don't want yours in their yard. Some people just aren't huggers. Talk on your cell phone in the presence of others only when absolutely necessary.

Make it your goal to never be called rude. Yield to others in traffic, take your arguments outside, and remember that the customer service person you're so mad at has a family too.

You may live like you're an island, but you're much closer to land than you realize. Care enough about others that you show them proper respect.

"Do to others as you would have them do to you." —Luke 6:31

Excuse Me!

Of course, there will be times when you'll make an error in judgment. You'll burp in public. You'll interrupt someone in conversation. The commonly expected response at these times is, "Excuse me!"

Perhaps you don't think you should need to be excused for someone else's trivial expectations. But what you define as trivial others consider significant. And if you're looking to become a better human being, that should matter.

Our society loves those who rebel against the status quo and cultural norms. But every culture has norms. And everyone has a way they like to be treated. So the issue isn't whether you understand or agree with a cultural expectation; it's whether you want to understand and honor other human beings.

Good manners are an easy way to honor others. Asking their pardon when you offend their expectations is another.

Do not cause anyone to stumble . . . even as I try to please everyone in every way. —1 Corinthians 10:32–33

From Enforcing to Affirming

As you make good manners more of a lifestyle, there is a danger to be aware of. The more seriously you take your manners, the more you'll be tempted to judge others who don't. The problem with that is that condemning others for their bad manners is just another form of bad manners.

It's not up to you to enforce the good manners of others. However, it is helpful to affirm them. Practicing good manners isn't just about being polite; it's about affirming what's best in others. Affirm a person's value, and your good manners will be affirmed as well. And they may just start following suit.

People are always watching what you do. So be consistent in practicing good manners. Make it clear that you don't do it out of obligation but because you care about what matters. That example will always speak louder than words.

"Let your light shine before others, that they may see your good deeds and glorify your Father in heaven." —Matthew 5:16

Earning Your Merit Badge

The Scouts are known for both good deeds and good manners. The Boy Scout law states that "a Scout is trustworthy, loyal, helpful, friendly, courteous, kind, obedient, cheerful, thrifty, brave, clean, and reverent." This has led to calling someone who always wants to do the right thing a *Boy Scout*.

The world could use more Boy Scouts and Girl Scouts. In a culture that celebrates selfishness above courtesy, perhaps we could all stand to crack open the Scout manual to remember what it means to care more for others than for ourselves.

Seeking to improve your manners will show others, as well as yourself, that people deserve your respect. Learning their customs and expectations, watching your bearing, asking for pardon when you fail—these are all the marks of someone on the road to becoming a better human being.

The merit badge for good manners is there for the taking. Go out and earn it.

"By this everyone will know that you are my disciples, if you love one another." —John 13:35

What You Leave Behind

How do you want to leave this earth?

With four cars in the driveway? A wall of college degrees, proving all your accumulated knowledge? A treasury of money and investments the size of Fort Knox?

Like the most powerful, richest civilizations of ancient Egypt and Rome, all the things you've accumulated will one day be bits of stone and dust. What will outlast you—both in the generations that follow and in the life beyond—is not what you collect but what you give.

What you give of your time, your money, your talents, your knowledge—this can be your lasting heritage. What you give will both empty and fill you. It will challenge and refine you. It will mold you into becoming a human being of true worth and substance.

You can start making your plans for departure now. Plan to leave this earth with nothing to show but a legacy that matters.

We make a living by what we get. We make a life by what we give.
—anonymous

What You Accumulate

If the love of money is the root of all evil, then perhaps giving away your money is the root of all good. If not, it's certainly one of the great goods in this world.

There are few better feelings than giving to those in need—the poor, the orphan, a relative, or a friend in dire straits. Or giving to those making a difference in what matters—your church, charitable organizations, a missionary or aid worker.

We're told to build wealth with accumulation in mind. While it is wise to earn, budget, and save, don't do it so you can have more and more. Do it so you'll have enough financial security to give away as much as possible.

By giving away your money, you do accumulate something—a closer connection to the Source of all that matters and a sense that you played a part in sharing the best kind of wealth with those in need.

One person gives freely, yet gains even more; another withholds unduly, but comes to poverty. —Proverbs 11:24

Your Most Precious Commodity

When people want to become better, one of the first things they learn to do is budget their money. One of the next steps is learning how to budget and prioritize their time.

Why? Is it so they'll have more peace and security from the pressures of the world? That's certainly one good reason to do it. Just like one of the main reasons to accumulate wealth is to give more of it away, it is also one of the best reasons to prioritize your time.

More than money, time may be your most precious commodity. Your kid asks for a bigger allowance, but what he really needs is more time with you. You and your spouse would probably argue less about money if you invested more time in each other's love accounts.

The more time you give to the things that matter, the richer your life will be.

Be very careful, then, how you live—not as unwise but as wise, making the most of every opportunity. —Ephesians 5:15—16

The Gift of Dirt and Sweat

Imagine yourself in a hole, covered in dirt, gripping a shovel in both hands. You strike hard into the earth and then lift the shovel, dropping the dirt onto a rising pile above. You look down, take a breath, then dig again.

What's your motivation to dig? If you're digging for a paycheck, there's certainly some reward. If it's to improve your home, your motivation may rise. But if you're digging for someone in need, someone who can't dig for himself, then your heart for the work should feel different altogether.

No one likes getting too close to someone covered in dirt and sweat. But if the dirt and sweat are the product of kindness and love, then there's no more beautiful sight to see.

Work for a paycheck. Work for family and home. But also labor for those who can only respond in gratitude. Each drop of sweat will be all the payment you need.

In everything I did, I showed you that by this kind of hard work we must help the weak. —Acts 20:35

The Need to Know

Who was your favorite teacher? Maybe it was the person who taught you piano. Or a high school science teacher or that literature professor. Some would say their mother. Some would speak of a mentor or a spiritual counselor.

Hopefully the knowledge you've accumulated has benefited you. You've learned a trade and now earn a living. You have wisdom to avoid life's pitfalls and to enjoy life's pleasures. But is that the only purpose your knowledge serves?

The ultimate end for your knowledge and wisdom should be to pass it on to others. It doesn't matter how smart you think you are. What matters is that you possess bits of fact, pieces of advice, lessons from experience that are too valuable to keep to yourself.

Your best teachers have made you who you are. In the knowledge you share with others, you can return the favor for those with a need to know.

Wisdom is a shelter as money is a shelter, but the advantage of knowledge is this: Wisdom preserves those who have it.
—Ecclesiastes 7:12

Look Behind You

Some people are born leaders. The rest of us need to learn that we've been leaders all along.

Leading simply means that anyone would look at what you're doing, saying, or thinking and want to do likewise. People are always watching. Most are looking to follow somebody. Look behind you. There's probably somebody back there.

Whether we admit it or not, we're always craving guidance for our next steps and are influenced by those we see. So give others the gift of your leadership. Walk in a way that you'd want your children to follow. Be an example that your family and friends would model.

Your life is a gift—not just the fact that you're alive but the way you live. That can be your gift to others. Make your life a gift to those who are starving for something more.

Join together in following my example, brothers and sisters, and just as you have us as a model, keep your eyes on those who live as we do. —Philippians 3:17

Spend What You Have

Why would anyone give his or her life for another? We watch flag-draped caskets arriving home from overseas. People actually gave their lives for our country. We trumpet words like *freedom* and *patriotism*, but it still seems like such a high price to pay. Would we do it?

The Christian faith is founded on the fact that God's Son gave His life for humankind. It's so often mentioned that it almost loses its meaning. Why would anyone give her life for others in such a way? Would we?

You may not have to give your life in the way soldiers or saviors do, but you can give your money, your time, your sweat, your wisdom, and your guidance. It makes no sense in the world's understanding that in emptying yourself you'll find fulfillment. But it's true.

Give of what you have, and you'll become who you're meant to be—a person of eternal wealth and riches beyond imagining.

"It is more blessed to give than to receive." —Acts 20:35

section

What Freedom Really Is

Look at a homeless man sometime. You'd think he was free. He probably doesn't have a job he has to report to. He doesn't have to answer to anyone or be anywhere. He's essentially free to do whatever he wants.

But when you look into his eyes, there's likely also an emptiness, a mix of pain and a numbed reality. He's frozen in hopelessness. He sighs in weariness and despair. So how free is he really?

How can we be free to do what we like and still be in bondage? Perhaps freedom isn't just about what we can choose to do but also about what consequences result from our choices.

And also this: true freedom isn't ultimately defined by how many options we have but by who we are inside. And that kind of freedom is only discovered when our choices move beyond superficial self-interest to decisions governed by the life that matters.

Jesus said, "If you hold to my teaching, you are really my disciples. Then you will know the truth, and the truth will set you free."
—John 8:31–32

The Bonds of Promise

Sadly, families suffer from the world's idea of freedom. Marital unfaithfulness abounds. Fewer people are getting married at all. The freedom to choose who you're with has become more important than sticking it out for a lifetime.

This desire to be free creates more bondage still. Second and third marriages fail much quicker. Unmarried couples rarely stay together long. Children know little more than brokenness and continue the pattern.

In marriage and in all things, the life that matters is usually the opposite of your carnal instincts. The bonds of promise are the only thing that will ever free you from the consequences of self-destructive desire.

But no matter where your choices or the choices of others have left you, the freedom of lifelong promise can still be yours. You need to believe that this is where your freedom lies and trust that God can make you whole again.

"So if the Son sets you free, you will be free indeed." —John 8:36

Independence for Your Soul

On a warm day in July, America sets out blankets and fires up barbecues to celebrate the moment our Founding Fathers proclaimed that they had a God-given right to be free from the tyrannies of England.

We are now free to worship, to speak our minds, and to live where we like. And that matters. But there are other tyrannies that still imprison us: prejudice, hatred, selfishness, guilt, depression, recklessness. As Americans, we may seem to be perfectly free but still walk in hopeless bondage.

When it comes to such deeper areas of oppression, it's important to separate our ideas of political freedom from emotional and spiritual freedom. Only God can help us rise out of our selfishness and pain to truly walk in the freedom that comes from within.

As Americans, we are free to govern ourselves. But our souls can only be free when they're governed by God.

It is for freedom that Christ has set us free. —Galatians 5:1

Trading One Master for Another

The word *slave* isn't exactly pleasant to our modern ears. It's linked to a horrible history. Human beings were kidnapped and made to live in forced labor at the hands of cruel masters.

While this type of slavery has always existed, the concept once had a broader scope. In ancient times, a slave could also be someone who worked to pay off a debt or to make payment for a crime.

When it comes to our freedom, the Bible addresses both types of slavery. Our sinful compulsions are a cruel master we didn't choose to serve. However, we get to choose God. And He is a good Master. He still controls us, but it's our choice to have Him do so. This choice leads to our freedom.

It may not feel very American to think that anyone should be your master, but this is the key to freeing yourself from your enslavement to a life that doesn't matter.

Now that you have been set free from sin and have become slaves to God, the benefit you reap leads to holiness, and the result is eternal life. —Romans 6:22

Freedom For . . .

Most people want to be free *from* something, like an unhealthy relationship or a destructive habit.

But usually what enslaved you was an unmet need: a woman desires love but suffers one abusive relationship after another; a man wants freedom from pain but goes from one addiction to another. Being free from bondage for a time doesn't fill the vacuum of underlying need.

So the second phase of freedom, which actually finishes the job, is to be free *for* something else—the thing that actually meets the need you've been searching for.

The woman must know she's worthy of God's love and then use that freedom to find a man who loves her like God does. The man needs to discover the freedom of God's peace and pursue genuine and lasting healing from his pain.

Once you're free from what's destroying you, you must live for what gives you life or you'll never truly be free.

You, my brothers and sisters, were called to be free. But do not use your freedom to indulge the flesh; rather, serve one another humbly in love. —Galatians 5:13

Preserving Your Freedom

Turn on cable news these days and very often you'll hear debates about preserving our freedoms. These debates are warranted. History shows that when we take a passive stance toward freedom, someone almost always comes to take it away.

Once you start walking in God's freedom, you must also take similar precautions. When you're freed of anything, it's easy to let down your guard. You're so happy to be liberated from what held you that you're ready to take a nice quiet vacation.

But the tyrant who would enslave you once again is waiting for that opening, and he will pounce when you're not aware. So take him seriously. The tyrant is your old life of selfishness and sin.

Live joyfully in the freedom God gives you, but always keep one eye open for the enemy. Don't give him an inch of territory as you preserve the freedom that matters.

It is for freedom that Christ has set us free. Stand firm, then, and do not let yourselves be burdened again by a yoke of slavery.
—Galatians 5:1

The Freedom to Choose

In the movie *Saving Private Ryan*, Ryan watches a man dying at his feet. The dying man has traveled through war-torn country to find him and to make sure he gets home to his family. He's accomplished his task but has given his life to do so. His last words to Ryan are, "Earn this."

What would you do if someone gave his life for you in this way? You'd probably feel compelled to make something of yourself. To make choices that matter. After all, your life was bought with a price.

The freedom that matters was also bought with a price. God's Son traveled through war-torn country to find you and died so you could live in freedom. You can't earn this kind of freedom, but you can live in a way that honors the One who gave it to you.

You've been given the freedom to choose. Live for yourself or live for Him.

For Christ's love compels us. . . . He died for all, that those who live should no longer live for themselves but for him who died for them and was raised again. —2 Corinthians 5:14–15

Cling with All Your Might

How we become better human beings both begins and ends with faithfulness. God has faith in us when we don't believe in ourselves. He reaches down and calls us to become people who matter.

If we're smart, we'll have faith that such change is possible. We'll start to believe that He really loves us, that He knows how best to shape our character and order our lives. When we're burdened by weariness and doubt, we'll remember His faithfulness. And we'll push on toward the finish line.

Why does faithfulness matter? Faithfulness matters because without faith, there is no trust; without trust, there is no connection; without connection, there is no relationship; and without relationship, there is no life. Without life, nothing matters.

Believe only in the One who believes in you, and you can remain faithful to the end. Cling with all your might to the life that matters.

Know therefore that the LORD your God is God; he is the faithful God, keeping his covenant of love to a thousand generations of those who love him and keep his commandments.

—Deuteronomy 7:9

Small Tests of Faithfulness

Military trainees are given precise instructions in storing their T-shirts and other clothes. A T-shirt must be folded into a long rectangle, then rolled tightly in a careful manner so that there is a perfect, unwrinkled product at the end.

What does this have to do with soldiering? If a trainee can't follow such simple, detailed instructions, how can he ever be trusted to operate a rifle or a tank in the heat of battle? Faithfulness in the little things is seen as preparation for the big ones.

Every day, you're given small tests of your faithfulness: showing up on time, keeping your promises, obeying your superiors. These may not seem like much, but they are your best preparation for staying the course in the heat of battle.

By staying faithful in the small things, you'll lay a foundation for faithfulness when it really matters.

"He who is faithful in what is least is faithful also in much; and he who is unjust in what is least is unjust also in much."
—Luke 16:10 *NKJV*

The Beginning Is
Also the End

It's funny how quickly we can lose sight of what matters. You start off strong but are lured away by the trinkets of superficial living.

Of course, faltering simply means we're human, so you shouldn't condemn yourself. But one key to remaining faithful to what matters is to remember where it all comes from in the first place.

Indeed, God is the source. He set all that matters in motion, and He is guiding it along the way. He is called the alpha and omega, both the beginning and the end. He was the first cause of your desire to pursue what matters. Ultimately, it will be up Him to move your desire to action, your action to perseverance, and your perseverance to completion.

None of us is absolutely faithful. Only God is. So the only way to become more faithful to what matters is to stay connected to the Source of all faithfulness.

Being confident of this, that he who began a good work in you will carry it on to completion until the day of Christ Jesus.
—Philippians 1:6

Fix Your Eyes

When you want to accomplish something, nothing beats a living example. Read all the books, take all the classes, learn from the best teachers, but until you actually meet someone who's done it, it'll never seem possible.

God's Son walked in the same human weakness. He faced the same temptations, the same opposition, yet He made it through to the end. Did he accomplish that by using His heavenly superpowers? No. He trusted in His Father.

In remaining faithful to what matters, your job is less to strive than to trust. God will strengthen you in your weakness and temptation. He will have your back when others try to stop you.

Hopefully you've already met the Man who has done what you're trying to accomplish in living a life that matters. Fix your eyes on Him as you press on toward the goal.

Fixing our eyes on Jesus, the pioneer and perfecter of faith. For the joy set before him he endured the cross. . . . Consider him who endured such opposition from sinners, so that you will not grow weary and lose heart. —Hebrews 12:2–3

Get Back Up

It's not real.

You've been unfaithful. You've broken too many promises. You've been betrayed by those you trusted. You wonder if you've just been duped. Maybe all this talk of what matters has all been a lie. Maybe there's no God at all.

But God is still in heaven. He is watching you. He hurts that you are hurting. He mourns for your pain. He sorrows for your hopelessness. He's waiting though. He won't press you. He wants you to see the truth for yourself.

There is no pit that the hand of the Almighty can't lift you out of—hopelessness, brokenness, or despair. Even if you've turned your back on Him or the life that matters, He is still faithful.

God is calling you with the sound of a gentle whisper: *Get back up. I'm here. Come walk with Me again.*

It is not the end. Get back up.

The LORD gives victory to his anointed. He answers him from his heavenly sanctuary with the victorious power of his right hand.
—*Psalm 20:6*

Only Remember

Recall the times God was faithful.

There's no way you should have missed that car when it spun out of control, but you did. Your child was so sick. The doctors prepared you for the worst. And then, one day, she was better. You were ready to give up on living when a friend turned up out of the blue, and somehow, everything changed.

Part of stopping to embrace what matters is recognizing a miracle when you see it. From the biggest miracles to the tiniest graces, God is at work on your behalf. Life itself is a miracle to be enjoyed.

But how easily we forget! That's why jogging your memory with the times God has intervened will give you fuel to remain faithful. The Bible is a catalog of memories that can encourage you too.

Remember what He has done. Stick around to see what else He might do.

But be sure to fear the LORD and serve him faithfully with all your heart; consider what great things he has done for you.
—1 Samuel 12:24

The Greatest Thing

The mark of your faithfulness will ultimately be seen in one thing, the greatest thing: how well you have loved God and others.

You live in fear and doubt. *Love* always believes.

You break your promises and betray your family and friends. *Love* always trusts.

You run away from God and the companions you most need. *Love* restores and connects.

You go your own way and despair that your life will ever matter. *Love* invites you to return.

Although love isn't the only thing, it is the greatest thing. Your life matters because even when you feel the most unworthy, you are loved. Your life matters because even when you've known only brokenness, you can learn to love again.

Love is bigger than all of us. That's the whole point. Remain faithful to your love for God, His love for you, and your love for others, and everything else will truly matter.

[Love] always protects, always trusts, always hopes, always perseveres. Love never fails. —1 Corinthians 13:7–8

CONCLUSION

Breathe It In

Take the deepest breath. What can you smell? The mint from your herb garden? A casserole cooking to perfection? Brewing coffee? Fresh-cut grass? The miraculous scent of a rose?

What else passes through your senses? Perhaps it's the laughter of children at play. The knowing look from a friend. The tingle of love when your spouse caresses your arm.

Breathe in again. What enters your soul? Hopefully it is a peace with who you are and why you're here. An insight into life's mysteries. A connection to God and nature and humankind. A freedom from the drudgery of superficial living. A drive to become more than who you are today.

The clock ticks with a similar rhythm to life's breath. But when you breathe this deeply, time seems to slow and even to stop.

Stop and take notice of the things that really matter. Breathe in and breathe out. Live life to the fullest!

When they had all had enough to eat, he said to his disciples,
"Gather the pieces that are left over. Let nothing be wasted."
—John 6:12

Notes

Notes

_____

_____

_____

_____

_____

_____

_____

_____

_____

_____

_____

_____

_____

_____

_____

_____

_____

_____

Notes

_____

_____

_____

_____

_____

_____

_____

_____

_____

_____

_____

_____

_____

_____

_____

_____

Notes

Notes

Notes

_____

_____

_____

_____

_____

_____

_____

_____

_____

_____

_____

_____

_____

_____

_____

_____

_____

_____

Notes

_____

_____

_____

_____

_____

_____

_____

_____

_____

_____

_____

_____

_____

_____

_____

Notes

Notes

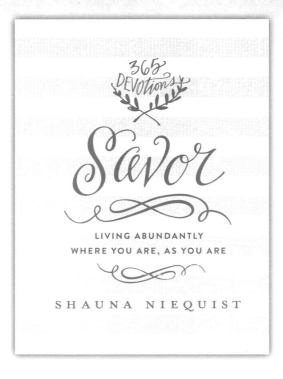

365 DEVOTIONS

Savor

LIVING ABUNDANTLY
WHERE YOU ARE, AS YOU ARE

SHAUNA NIEQUIST

Let's savor this day, the beauty of the
world God made, the richness of family
and friendship, and the good gifts of
creativity and work. Let's walk together.

The new 365-day devotional from
Shauna Niequist!

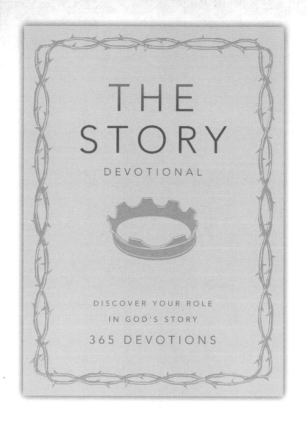

THE
STORY

DEVOTIONAL

DISCOVER YOUR ROLE
IN GOD'S STORY

365 DEVOTIONS

FIND YOUR PLACE IN
GOD'S EPIC STORY.

Spend each day reading God's story, and
let Him be the author of your life.